GRANDPARENTS DON'T JUST BABYSIT

GRANDPARENTS DON'T JUST BABYSIT

RUTH ISBISTER

DENEAU

1989

Deneau Publishers
760 Bathurst Street
Toronto, Ontario
M5S 2R6

Illustrations and cover art by Pam Pfohl

Printed and bound in Canada

Canadian Cataloguing in Publication Data

Isbister, Ruth, 1913–
Grandparents Don't Just Babysit

ISBN 0-88879-206-9

1. Grandparent and child. 2. Family.
3. Grandparents – Family relationships.
I. Title.

HQ759.9.I82 1989 306.8′7 C89-093607-2

Dedicated to: my grandmother Nixon and to Victoria, David, Simon, Peter, Ian, Jane and David.

Contents

Acknowledgments

In the course of writing this book, I interviewed and corresponded with friends and acquaintances who are grandparents, parents and grandchildren. They live in various parts of Canada and the United States, and a few of them are in the United Kingdom. They numbered about a hundred and were generous with their time and views. They also gave substance to the subject matter: they shaped and expanded my ideas. I am indebted to each of them. I have avoided identifying them by name.

Among those who clarified my thinking in the early stages were Margaret Kidd, June Engel and Katherine Morrison. Special thanks to Roz Spafford, teacher, editor, writer and also my daughter-in-law, who worked solidly with me for a short period of time in California, and gave me confidence by the way she whipped the drafts into shape. And special thanks to Jennifer Glossop, my editor, who has the perception to help make clear what I am trying to say.

Our three children John, Alex and Katie were always available for me to consult. My husband helped immeasurably, and he insists that I say nothing about it.

Introduction

This book is about grandparents and their relationships with their grandchildren. All of us have grandparents, although some of us don't know them, and most of us become grandparents. And yet the grandparent-grandchild relationship—so essential to the family—has not been paid the kind of attention that the parent-child relationship has.

It is possible to fail at grandparenting, but failure is not necessary. The obstacles to good relationships are many: too much distance and too little time are the most common. Many grandparents are uncertain about how to reach out to their grandchildren. The generation gap seems like an abyss. Others find that their own situation or that of their children gets in the way. Yet being a grandparent is so enjoyable and rewarding that it is worth the work and care necessary to get it right. This book will, I hope, help you avoid some of the stumbling blocks and build a sound and satisfying relationship with your grandchildren.

In addition to the basics required to understand and deal with children, I will be considering some of the changes in our society that have made grandparenting today more challenging. Technological and economic forces have radically altered our social structures, including the family unit. The circumstances in which families find themselves are very different from conditions in other times. Many people today live far from the land in which they were raised. Most of them left their older family members behind, and only a few have lived long with grandparents or have known them in a stable environment.

In earlier times the family was a larger, closely knit economic unit. The necessities for family survival often included three generations living in close proximity. People's life spans were shorter, but they had time and scope for a mutual support system. Bonding was strong, and grandparents played an important role in guiding and supporting the younger members of the family. They were powerful figures who passed down wisdom from generation to generation. Today the generations are not together long enough to talk about recipes—let alone tradition.

I was brought up in Toronto in a traditional setting with a large family network. We had close ties. All the family, including eventually three great-grandchildren, gathered for Sunday dinners and birthday picnics. "The duplex" was a large house with one set of cousins upstairs and one set down. Grandma and Grandpa had their living room and kitchen downstairs and their bedroom upstairs; they were the focus of family get-togethers. We lived a few blocks away and could drop in any time. There was a sense of belonging and a place to run to. Grandma had time for each and every one of us.

My husband had a large connection of relatives. Before radio and television, people gathered in one of the family houses, and they would entertain each other. Someone would play the piano or another instrument, and everyone would sing. Three generations would enjoy themselves together, and the relationships were very direct and personal.

Today large and stable families in this pattern are in the minority. Family members tend to find themselves separated from one another, whether by choice or by necessity. Both parents are more and more frequently engaged in earning the family's income. Keeping in contact, even with one's spouse, takes planning. Grandparents, too, are often in the work force. These new developments in the family scene tend to isolate members from each other and test the handling of the young child's basic needs.

Just as parenting is a task that has to be learned and often approached with some misgiving, so grandparenting is a learning process and reveals unsuspected dilemmas and ineptitudes. We grope for new relationships with our children in their role as parents. Our life-styles may be very different. The job of grandparenting may appear to be a heavy load, but it's worth it.

The rewards are great, but they cannot be bought, bribed or cajoled. There is no way around it; we must treat grandchildren as people in their own right. Why do we take the trouble? The answer is so simple that it is almost embarrassing. The clue is a pair of eyes—welcoming, confident, unwavering and smiling—a grandchild who is genuinely glad we are there. In short, this is love. This is what it is all about.

1

Being a Grandparent

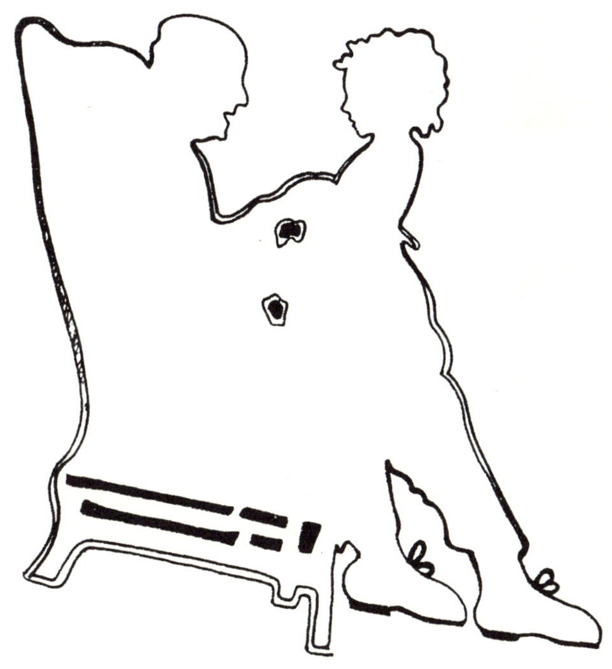

Grandparents occur freely in nature, and it is easy to become one. There it is in the Old Testament: Abraham begat Isaac. When Isaac begat Jacob, Abraham became a grandfather. Two begats make a grandparent, and everybody has or had at least four.

Our role

The fundamental roles of grandparents remain the same even while the superficial patterns of society change. For a grandparent, the newly arrived baby is a delight in herself. She is also a confirmation of connection between past and future. She is an inescapable reality: "I loved her before she was born!" said one grandmother. That grandmother's deep feelings stem from her own experience of childbearing and her expectations for the new life. A desired pregnancy in a responsible relationship and a healthy birth bring forth a joyous affirmation. The news "Mother and baby doing well" is thrilling, be it your first grandchild or your fifth.

If your desire to have grandchildren is strong, chances are it is based on three elements: an attraction to children, a sense of self-fulfillment and an instinct about your biological line. You probably also have dreams about your grandchildren's achievements and about the grandparent-grandchild relationship that will develop.

What Grandparents Give To Grandchildren

Grandparents give a love that is freer than that of the parents. Grandparents do not burden a child with expectations to the extent that parents do. You have often heard it said that grandparents have all the fun and none of the responsibility.

There are qualities of mutual admiration between grandparent and grandchild that give the child and the grandparent a feeling of being special. You transfer a feeling of confidence to your grandchild as, hand in hand, you explore some new and intriguing interest of his. If we allow ourselves to become isolated from our grandchildren we deprive ourselves of an enrichment of our own lives and the lives of our grandchildren.

Children spend much of their time seeking their roots and establishing their identities—who am I and how do I fit into my world? Parents provide a child with roots, but grandparents provide deeper ones. By their presence grandparents add something to the child's comprehension of the continuity of life, the dimensions of time and human interrelatedness. Many grandparents excel at helping the younger generation make significant connections with the past. Children love stories about the old days. Do remember, though, that a little of this kind of thing goes a long way. Don't dwell on family history to the point of boredom. By the time you get to Aunt Donalda's relation to Uncle John's wife's sister, a normal and healthy grandchild tends to lose track of the plot.

I had a long walk with a young neighbor, Eric, age nine. He visits his family's ancestral home in Sweden every summer. I asked him whether they talked about what it was like on the farm when his father was little. "Yes," he said, "the difference is that things were done by hand then and today we have more electrical machines." He continued: "In the old days they trusted kids more. My dad and mom and aunts and uncles talk about all the great things they used to do. Grandpa let them take boats across the lake, go to music fetes and dances. Adults don't trust kids to do things on their own these days." When I asked him what he likes best about the visits, he replied: "I love the wonderful candy my grandmother makes."

Eric has a clear sense of the past, and his grandmother has certainly made an impression on him. He perceives that life was wonderful in his parents' childhood and people seemed more trusting—not an altogether wrong impression! Through these conversations Eric is clarifying his values as well as solidifying his identity. The immediate presence of Eric's family is not so important as the quality of their reunion each summer. His grandmother made it all possible.

Penny's grandmother told her a tale about her and her brother when they were young children. Penny remarked: "I loved it when Grandma told me that her brother used to tease her and pull her pigtails and that she got real mad at him. That's exactly the way I feel when my sister tells Mom stories on me! I get so mad!" Grandchildren are fascinated to realize that grandparents have weaknesses, too. They have more fun and identify more with grandparents who aren't on pedestals.

Something very important happened once when Penny had a talk with her grandmother. "Granny, do you know what? I miss Grandpa; I miss his jokes and his bushy eyebrows." Granny said: "I miss him, too, Penny, so much that I cry sometimes." Penny said: "Do you really? I didn't know grandmothers cried." When you start talking this way with a granddaughter you know you have made a solid connection. Penny is getting to know her grandmother better. Even more significant, she is at an age where she is experiencing emotions that are new to her. By telling her grandmother about them, she learns to understand them better.

Children want to know about their parents. Grandparents can provide them with glimpses of what their parents were once like. "Your dad helped me lay the floor in our cabin at the lake," said Grandpa Bill. "That's why he's so good at doing our kitchen floor!" said Johnny. He went on: "Grandpa, tell me that story again about my dad spilling the oil in the garage and trying to clean it up with Grandma's mop."

Young Simon loved to hear about his father's growing-up years, and he repeated the stories often. "My grandparents tell such neat stories about my dad when he was just a kid," said Simon to a friend. "My dad used to play on a soccer team. When my grandparents were watching a final game at the school, the seat of Dad's trousers split and he didn't know it. He was twelve, and I guess he was growing out of his clothes like I am now and, pop, they went."

Letting our grandchildren dip into our past puts them in touch with us and with their parents. Some grandparents may not be aware that the knickknacks from the past, lying around in their houses, are treasures to be explored. The holiday souvenirs, the piano with the old songbook on the stand, the wonderful stuff that wasn't thrown away—these are the ingredients that make a heritage. It has little to do with material value or wealth, but rather with belonging. Your granddaughter finds her mom's old riding hat and some false eyelashes in a box, and she registers the memory forever. I know a granddaughter who treasures the gift of a magnifying glass that belonged to her grandmother.

Grandparents can give grandchildren support and identity. "Here comes my grandma to take me home," shouts Danny at the window of his nursery school. A grandchild doesn't often say, "Thank you, Grandma," but the squeeze of his warm hand in yours is appreciation enough.

Love is the common element that underlies all the caring, sharing and giving. Children need to be looked after and they need to know they are loved. Secure in this knowledge of love a child can go on to establish and sort out his own unique emotions.

Many children learn about compassion, concern and loss when one of their grandparents approaches the inevitable end. When my friend Michael came to Toronto from Ottawa to visit his mother in a nursing home, he decided to bring his nine-year-old son. Michael's son realized that his grandmother had changed a great deal. Her eyes still twinkled, but she was physically frail and much less coherent. After the visit he showed concern and anxiety and he wanted to talk to his dad. Michael explained to him that Grandma was very old and would probably not live much longer; that we all must die and life was like that. He reminded his son of the many wonderful memories they had of Grandma—how bright she had been, and all the fun and fine times they had had together. They would remember that and lots more about their past with her.

Michael was not telling his son how to feel or how to express his emotions, rather he was providing his son with a wonderful opportunity to develop. The feelings revealed and exchanged between these two people will become part of their common heritage. It is one more precious gift from Grandma to both of them.

What Grandparents Get From Grandchildren

Grandchildren have a knack of making us feel needed and wanted. Most grandparents, I think, find that this is what they want most from the relationships with their grandchildren. As we get older our connections with people who are important to us become fewer and more distant. We want very much to be needed now, even though nothing can diminish the memories and significance of our past experiences.

Do you have friends who take relaxing pills and count to ten instead of exploding? Has your doctor talked to you about reducing your tensions? Your grandchild teaches you to play again, and playing is a great restorative.

Our grandchildren also teach us how to shed our protective coverings—our rigidities and seeming disinterest. We cannot really get to know a baby without getting down on the floor with him, making eye contact and playing his game, whether it is rolling a ball, clapping hands or peekaboo. If we have unintentionally become an old fogy, we need to rediscover the fun of being a companion and a pal. Our grandchildren teach us to listen, observe and share. We learn new arts by letting them explain their games. We enter again into the age-old drama of storytelling by listening—sometimes at great length—to what they found in a book or a movie.

Being a grandparent was described in a charming essay written by a ten-year-old. Several people showed me the same text, which has been circulated widely. I reproduce it without acknowledgment because I have been unable to identify the author.

WHAT IS A GRANDMOTHER?

> A grandmother is a lady who has no children of her own so she likes other people's little girls. A grandfather is a man grandmother. He goes for walks with the boys, and they talk about fishing and tractors, and things like that. Grandmothers don't have to do anything except be there. They're old, so they shouldn't play hard or run. It is enough if they drive us to the market where the pretend horse is and have lots of dimes ready. Or, if they take

> us for walks, they should slow down past things like pretty leaves and caterpillars. They should never say "Hurry up!"
>
> Usually they are fat, but not too fat to tie kids' shoes. They wear glasses and funny underwear. They can take their teeth and gums off.
>
> It's better if they don't typewrite or play cards except with us. They don't have to be smart, only answer questions like why dogs hate cats, and how come God isn't married. They don't talk baby talk like visitors do because it is hard to understand. When they read to us, they don't skip or mind if it is the same story again.
>
> Everybody should try to have one, especially if you don't have television, because grandmothers are the only grown-ups who have got time.

The grandparent-grandchild relationship is often terminated in an arbitrary way following a difficult divorce or misunderstanding. When access is denied it can be a cruel blow to the grandparents and an unfortunate deprivation for the children. Those of us who enjoy close connections with our children and grandchildren are lucky. The rewards are immediate and long-lasting.

What Parents Get From Grandparents

Everyone is the child of his or her parents, born of them with their genes, nurtured and directed by them. In this broad sense the story starts long before the birth of a grandchild. Every living person has been formed in large part by her parents in terms of habits, morality and attitudes. Not everyone becomes a carbon copy of her parents. Many rebel against their parents and try to be as different as possible. In these instances, however, the influence of the parents is still strong. When a daughter swears she will not take after her father, she is inescapably using him as a model.

How grandparents get along with their children will certainly affect how they relate to their grandchild. If the relationship wore thin some time ago, it may have to be patched before grandparenting can begin. If the grandparents don't get along with their daughter-in-law or son-in-law, they may have trouble feeling comfortable visiting their grandchild. An old joke comes to mind: "Isn't it amazing that the man who wasn't good enough for your daughter produced the best grandchild in the world."

The transfer of confidence and emotional support is the biggest contribution grandparents can make to the parents. Each passing year raises new questions for the parents. Grandparents who, after all, have been through this before, can make their knowledge and experience available, but the vibrations have to be right. Parents still bear the primary responsibility for nurturing and directing the children. Grandparents should not assume this responsibility except in dire emergency. Our role is an advisory one. We should be on tap but not on top.

On a more mundane level, parents know that, if they are available, grandparents are the best baby-sitters. When a child is sick and both parents are due at work, who better to phone than a grandparent? If grandfather and grandson are on good terms they can enjoy themselves raking the lawn or taking the furnace apart. When a young mother is preparing for a birthday party she can hardly forget to ask grandmother to make the best ever cake.

Money comes into it, too. Grandparents and parents often worry whether the children will get at least as good a start as they did. Most parents want to pay their own way, but this is not always possible. Whether the grandparents provide a young family with continuing financial support, most of them will stretch themselves to contribute what they can when unpredictable needs arise. (We return to this in more detail in Chapter Ten, which is about money.)

When trouble strikes—whether it is a divorce or a lost job or a sick child—grandparents can be of great personal help to the parents. These are times when parents come to rely on grandparents emotionally and sometimes financially. At such times grandparents can also provide a stable point in a grandchild's turbulent world.

Even grandparents who live far away or are busy with their own lives can remain relevant to family life, however. We have certainly not reached the stage of the disposable grandparent.

Health and Longevity

Some grandparents are younger than others and some in better shape than others. On the average, however, our health is stronger and our age span longer than it used to be. We are continuing into later years with enough vigor to flock to the YMCA, the golf course and the tennis club, to play bingo and bridge and do volunteer work. We may not always remember exactly where we laid down our purses or parked our cars, but never mind. In our youth—some time ago—we were more accustomed to grandparents who were slow or bedridden. Today more seniors are thoroughly enjoying the later years.

Since we are so active it might be thought that grandparents are more available to grandchildren than before, but it does not always work this way. Some of the avocations that attract grandparents do not attract children. A recreational program designed to meet the needs of seniors is quite probably too regimented for a child. There is no reason to expect a seven-year-old to care what goes on at a bridge table. Children are very spontaneous, and the most successful grandparents are those who still know how to find fun in the ordinary things that are under our noses.

Grandparents are entitled to remember that they are not twenty-three and, indeed, that they haven't been for some time now. Whatever our actual ages the chances are that our energy runs out sooner than it once did. When we are with children, we should keep in mind that tired can mean cranky and unresponsive—for both the child and the grandparent. Rather than forcing ourselves to keep going, we do better to spell ourselves off for a while and retreat. But it is best if we explain why we need to nap or to be alone. A break can calm the children, as well. As we all know, children get tired, too, but they do it differently. They tend to run at full speed, then shift into frantic overdrive and finally collapse. We tend to get a sore back.

Ethics and Morality

When you are a grandparent and have lived fully, it can be assumed that you have established your own code of moral behavior. You may feel that it is your right—even your duty — to pass on the wisdom of your years.

There were times and places in which elders were considered to be the best authorities on the differences between good and bad, right and wrong. But, these days, when social and other changes are occurring at breathtaking speed, people in general do not necessarily expect the experience of seniors to contribute much to the solution of current problems.

You can recognize this trend as constructive without losing sight of the contribution that elders can make—namely, to insist that right and wrong should be on the agenda. How can a grandparent best do this? The key is to catch the opportunities as they come. Grandparents need to be ready to pick up on children as they discuss moral issues such as cheating in school, stealing candy from a counter or hurting animals.

Children learn by making mistakes, and older people survive by avoiding them. This is a big difference. We can see examples of it everywhere we look. A child learns to walk by indulging patiently in a series of daring adventures, each of which sends her tumbling. In sharp contrast, a grandfather picks his way carefully over an icy surface knowing that he had better not fall. Children learn the golf swing—that intricate and artificial antic—by methods different from those of adults. A youngster swings the golf club loosely and freely, finally taming the whole into the pattern of the full, fast and directed sweep. In sharp contrast, an adult usually learns the individual components of the swing—the stance, the follow-through and so forth—by rote, and finally integrates them into a more or less efficient swing.

Keep such differences in mind when you want to communicate effectively with children about their attitudes and behavior. Avoid laying down rigid rules for them on matters in which they can develop rules only by experimenting. I do not mean to imply that rules should be abandoned, but only that the wise grandparent should consider which are necessary and for what.

Morals are not learned from a book. A grandchild develops her moral sensitivities from two principal sources, her relationships with other people and her experiences of loving and being loved.

Onstage

Getting into grandparenting is like going to a play, although, with the latter, you usually have a say in whether you go. There is a large and varied cast, audience participation, mishaps along the way but mainly good endings. In a play the stage set creates an atmosphere and establishes limits within which the action takes place. Similarly there is a setting to modern grandparenting, which does much to establish rules for this particular life drama.

The curtain rises on a grandmother and a grandfather, nothing unusual about them, in the living room in their apartment. This grandma is not (repeat not) by a fireplace in a rocking chair with hairpins and knitting needles. Her name is May; she is smartly dressed and coiffed in case she needs to buzz off at short notice. She is sitting in a corner, at the telephone, dealing with a client who is interested in buying a house. Will is a few years older, and he is in pretty good shape. He is as retired as he will ever be and is involved at present in raising money for the outreach program of his church. Will is pretending not be impatient to get at the telephone. He is almost due at the curling rink. They have the air of well-being that results from exercise and a reasonably careful diet.

May and Will are a couple of very adaptable people. To look at them it would be difficult to guess that the pace of change at which they have lived is unprecedented. During their lives the world has gone through the greatest changes in recorded history, and they have had to keep up. They have lived in a comparatively affluent society but they remember what it was like to be poor. They probably were brought up in rural settings or in smaller towns. May's mother was a full-time housewife, but May and her generation of women are quite accustomed to working for pay.

May and Will have become accustomed to the presence of people with different languages, skin colors and religions. Now they participate in the age of instant electronic communications to everywhere. They see every country in the world on television news, images relayed by satellite. They get more information than they can handle.

When they were young, people still thought that wars were won by one side or the other. Like others of their generation, May and Will went through the trauma of realizing that another big war could mean a worldwide holocaust. They seldom discuss it, but the thought is there.

But if grandparents have learned and changed by enduring transition, children have come into the world as it is now. May's and Will's grandchildren take for granted the world as it is. They accept rapid communication, convenient ground transportation, air travel and more television screens as essentials of life. They never knew a preelectronic, preatomic world. Children are more up-to-date than their grandparents, but the range of their experience is narrower.

Differences of this kind have always existed between the generations, but the recent pace of change has made the gap wider. Grandparents see television as a barrier to literacy, and children see it as their main route to information. The grandson wants war games for Christmas, but May and Will disapprove. Both sides have their reasons and neither may be wrong but this does not resolve the questions. May and Will are flexible but they have aged and they have their limits. To keep in touch with their grandchildren entails continuous efforts on their part to understand where the children are, their motivations and their problems.

There is an art to being a grandparent. We tell our grandchildren about bridges to their past while they give us a glimpse of bridges to the future. We help them grow up while they help us be younger. They give us opportunities to know our own children better, in their roles as parents. We and our grandchildren provide each other with love.

2

It Takes All Kinds

My husband thinks a book on grandparenting, like books on economics or anthropology, should demonstrate at least some effort to be scientific. (He has a notion that economics is scientific, and I have not had the heart to disabuse him.) So I decided to classify grandparents, just as botanists classify plants.

I sent a questionnaire to a number of grandparents and interviewed others. With few exceptions these people were working at the job of being a grandparent. Running through most of their accounts were common themes of love, affection and family ties. Whatever the words, they all expressed a strong desire to maintain good relationships between the generations. There were, however, differences, and these tended to fall into certain patterns.

From these patterns I formed five major categories of grandparents. They are the Eager Beavers, the Widowed and Helpful, the Awkwards, the Cool Cucumbers and the No Problems. As is usual with new scientific breakthroughs, some of you will change and improve my categories, but I put mine forward for starters. Let's examine each in turn.

Eager Beavers

The Eager Beavers are usually grandmothers, though there are a few grandfathers. They are properly envied by others for the ease with which they pitch in and contribute helpfully. They are practical, energetic, hands-on folk who butter the sandwiches, do the telephoning, run the rummage sales and make things go in church socials, constituency organizations, clubs, meetings and in their grandchildren's families. They revel in being grandparents and recognize no stumbling blocks. No sane parent would want to get along without such a grandparent, but there are unfortunately not enough to go around.

Trudy is an Eager Beaver. She and her husband, Ralph, live a distance away from their grandchildren since they retired to a warmer town in the south. They value their vital connection with their grandchildren and they work at it. The young family comes to see them about twice a year. Trudy makes fairly frequent trips to their former city and usually stays in her daughter's home. The two families exchange letters and telephone calls and they enjoy the time they spend together.

I visited Trudy one afternoon when she was waiting for a phone call announcing the birth of their new grandson. (Her daughter had had amniocentesis and knew the baby was a boy.) Trudy was ready to fly at a moment's notice to see the family through the first couple of weeks with their new baby. "My prime motives for taking this long trip are family continuity and a love of kids," Trudy said.

Ralph was glad the newcomer was to be a boy although he said it made no real difference to him one way or the other. He made some speculative comments about his relationship with his new grandson. "What will he think of me if I'm hardly ever there? Will I be as close a friend to him as my grandfather was to me?" He knows, however, that Trudy will keep the connections strong.

Fred and Joan are Eager Beavers who throw themselves into activities that attract and involve the children. Both of them are sensitive to their adult son's needs. He has struggled through the breakdown of his first marriage and finds joy in making his second marriage work. Fred and Joan are ready to participate fully and happily as grandparents. They avoid barging in, but they help out a great deal. They feel they can contribute to their son's new family in important ways.

Knowing how much to help is sometimes a problem, though. Members of the genus Eager Beaver occasionally overreach, and these episodes can lead to touchy relationships, especially with daughters-in-law who are learning the ropes. One grandmother of our acquaintance, Alice, achieved the opposite of what she intended. She had read every word of Dr. Spock while having her own children and had lost track of the good books that had come along in the meantime. She had few doubts about child rearing and made her advice available too vigorously and too soon. Her daughter-in-law had already sought guidance elsewhere and intended to pursue it. Alice's point of view was not wrong in substance, but she kept missing the boat with regard to communication.

Alice expressed her concern more than once about a feeding problem that she thought was being mishandled. Her daughter-in-law felt she was being put down and that her competence as a mother was being challenged. Grandma Alice continues to visit, and she is made welcome, but the two feel less intimate.

New grandparents are in special danger of falling into this Eager Beaver trap. If they try to take over physically or psychologically it can be hard on young families, making them feel they are not trusted or are not mature enough to cope with parenting. But Eager Beavers can avoid these troubles, and many do. One of the secrets is to be slow to impose your own ideas while taking time to listen with respect to the parents and to your grandchild. (There is a good discussion of this problem in the book *Between Mothers-in-Law and Daughters-in-Law* by Helen S. Arnstein.) Grandparent discussion groups, led by a skilled leader in family life education, can also help us to see ourselves more clearly.

Many Eager Beavers get along best when they offer perspective instead of criticism. Grandmother Sylva is a master of the art of relieving pressures. She is at her best when her daughter-in-law is at her wit's end, impatient and angry with an out-of-hand child. With her years of experience, Sylva can sometimes see that her grandchild is behaving normally for his age. By diverting his attention to something more appealing, she can restore him to in-bounds behavior and keep Mom from wanting to throttle him.

Sylva is the kind of Eager Beaver who says: "It feels good to restore peace. So I do a diaper change and clear up the dishes. I love it! My idea of grandparenting is to give Wendy and Paul some relief from their two kids and give my grandchildren some relief from their parents." Sylva adds, "And a bit of cooking never hurts, since Wendy is often pressed for time to make nourishing meals." One day, however, Sylva found that this kind of help can backfire. Wendy said: "Please, Mom, easy on the casseroles. Paul is beginning to think I can't cook."

Popping in unexpectedly can become tricky when both parents work full-time. Wendy and Paul now employ a nanny because Wendy is back at work. Sylva says, "Nanny is very good and I don't like to disturb the peace, but I must say when I pick the three-year-old up and say to him, 'Grandma loves you so much,' I think I add a special something the sitter doesn't have." Sylva knows that she gets in the housekeeper's way if she drops in too frequently, but she and her husband, Leo, would like to do more to help. The situation calls for some good communication with regard to timing and schedules.

If you are an Eager Beaver, you probably derive great joy from your grandchildren. In all probability you are connected closely and actively with the people you love. Your family is lucky to have your help and love. But there is a little germ of danger. Beware that you may push too hard or wear out your welcome. If things start to go sour, seek an early opportunity for a frank discussion, and never hesitate to say you may have been wrong. Communication is the best way to reestablish good relations.

Widowed and Helpful

This category, which includes widowers as well as widows, is a special one, since those in it have had to adjust to two losses: the empty-nest syndrome after their children have left home and their grief after the death of their spouse. The lucky ones discover that the new joys of being a grandparent help them to sort out their lives again.

A veteran grandmother such as Barbara, for example, writes that she is having a wonderful time with her grandchildren. She says, "I consider grandmothering one of my most important activities at the moment." She shares her life in special ways with nine grandchildren, some of whose parents work full-time, some whose mothers are at home, some who live in the same community, and some who are farther away. She has avoided intruding on her children's households by entertaining her grandchildren at her house (which she still maintains). She has them over, one or two at a time, for meals, conversation and overnight stays. "Those living nearby come in often to sit in the kitchen or out in the garden just to talk." She is a nature lover and also takes the children on walks. They love to learn about the outdoors and have a good time collecting shells and leaves.

She writes: "The reason things have been working well for the past seventeen years is largely because of my own children and their spouses. They constantly give me a kind of buildup with their children, so that the children think I am really wonderful and super. Actually, they would probably like me anyhow. When our Kay was seven she told me in confidence that when she blew out the candles on her birthday cake she wished that I would never die."

Barbara found help some years ago in a magazine article. It said that a good grandmother is a person of great wisdom and few opinions. "I usually keep my opinions to myself unless they are good opinions," she said, "and I never criticize because it would not do the slightest good. I tell myself that there are many ways of bringing up children." (I did not presume to ask her how she decided which of her opinions were good enough to express.)

Barbara prefers to have the children visit one or two at a time. "I relate differently to each one. The eldest is seventeen. All I do, and really all I have ever done for him, is let him talk to me. He comes from a busy household. I make time to listen to him. He comes to supper once a week, usually arriving early. We sit in the backyard or he talks to me in the kitchen while I get supper. He talks fast, mostly about history, which is his greatest interest, but also about his friends or the members of his family or his religious beliefs.

"His brother is fourteen. Right now he lives in a world of his own. He is computer crazy and terribly good at chess. I am hopeless at games—I have never beaten him at anything, not even at ticktacktoe. But I have bought a number of books on games and puzzles and things, which I keep at my house so that he has something to amuse himself with when he comes here. Once I expressed my regret at the fact that I can't play difficult games with him, and he said: 'Well, that's true, Granny, but you are a super cook.'"

"Then there is little Mary, just turned twelve, competent at everything she touches, with much poise but overscheduled. I taught her how to knit and I encourage her to bring a friend over. About once or twice a year I take her to a movie or to something at the arts center. I think that probably the best thing I can do for her is to be a link between her and her cousin Ronnie, who lives in another city. Those two little cousins were born within three weeks of each other. They are both musical and play duets together on the piano, and on the flute and recorder. They are really very fond of each other, but they are very different and are being brought up completely differently. Their mothers don't get along too well and maintain that the children don't really like each other, but they do. So I try to establish a neutral meeting ground, because cousins are nice things to have when you grow up, especially for girls who don't have sisters. I have to be very careful not to arouse Mary's jealousy when Ronnie is here, because Ronnie only comes about twice a year and the visits are special. Mary I see every week. Two years ago Mary was so jealous it was quite a disaster, but now I think I know how to avoid this sort of thing."

As you can see, Barbara not only gives a lot of time but also much thought to her grandchildren. She recognizes their differences and the special contributions she makes to their lives. It is also clear that they appreciate her unique qualities.

Betty is a widowed grandmother I was lucky enough to catch on one of her visits from California. One of her sons lives in Winnipeg, and she visits his family for a few weeks each year. She then moves on to visit the other son and his family in Toronto. Betty invites the grandchildren to visit her two by two at Christmas, systematically pairing the cousins in turn. She says: "When my grandchildren come to California we really enjoy ourselves, especially our walks. As we stroll along the beach we get talking. Some of it is about me and some of it is about them. We laugh at how different things were those many years ago. I think they get a feeling from me —I hope they do—that I love doing simple things like walking barefoot, picking up shells and feeling the sun and wind. I find the children look forward to these walks. It's one way of catching up with each other and slowing down to a pace that allows for curiosity and questions." Betty is a spry seventy. She moves at a slow pace quite deliberately, and the children are grateful for it. It gives them time to poke into things. And like Barbara, she provides cousins with a chance to get to know each other and have time away from siblings and parents.

Deirdre is a widowed grandmother who lives close to her grandchildren, and they visit her frequently. Her son is divorced, has custody of his children and needs some help with child care. Deirdre likes to prepare meals and enjoys taking the children to a variety of types of entertainment—theater, ballet, movies. She says that hilarious things always happen when the children visit. "The other day," she told me, "I took my granddaughter to a special ballet performance. We were going down the aisle at intermission time; I had left my coat on my chair and suddenly looked down and found I was wearing my apron!" Deirdre loves her role. She is needed. Sometimes she finds it taxing but she spends a few mornings each week exercising and folk dancing at the Y, and she takes the odd trip away. She knows that she can't rely on her grandchildren to fill all the void in her life. She has other interests and pursues them actively.

Too much grandparent involvement can sour relationships, while too little deprives the family of nurturing. Out of this comes a golden rule for happy grandparenting: be on hand when you can be helpful; get lost when you are in the way—and don't sulk about it. The delicate balance of being welcome but not intruding is a vital art for grandparents.

Robin is a neophyte Widowed and Helpful who has learned this lesson quickly. She is alone. Her youngest son, Gordon, is married and successful in his job, and his family pattern is typical of many young upper-middle-class professionals. He and his wife, Tamara, both have jobs; they live in another part of the city and have two children, ages five and seven. Their lives are organized around the clock. They enjoy seeing Robin, but the pace of life makes visits difficult.

Robin finds keeping in touch a strain at times. When she ventures into their house, she finds an acceleration of activity, a sense of busyness that inhibits her comfortable participation.

And yet she finds it difficult to wait for them to call or visit. On many weekday mornings, Robin sits with her telephone in hand, looking at the clock, which says seven-thirty. Early morning is the only time she can be sure of reaching them, but she hesitates to call when they are the most rushed. She also avoids lengthy weekend visits at their house because Gordon and Tamara need time alone with their children and with each other.

Like other widowed grandparents, Robin has decided to do most of her grandparenting at her own home. She invites her grandchildren to visit her for the weekend, occasionally asking that they come one at a time. She feels that she is able to make a contribution by setting something of her own rhythm into their lives while at the same time having the opportunity to enjoy her grandchildren. She does not see Gordon as much as she would like, but she has learned not to expect him to solve her problems.

If you are a Widowed and Helpful, you have probably entered into close friendship with your grandchildren and you expect it to continue. You enjoy the time spent because you have developed common interests with them. It may well be that you do not see their parents as much as you would like, but the additional time grandparenting may compensate in part.

Awkwards

The Awkwards are warmhearted, and deep down they want to connect with their grandchildren. But they are not sure how to do it. They try and fail, and frustration mounts.

I have already referred to the scientific nature of my

observations. These led me to conclude that there are more men than women among the Awkwards. Although this conclusion seemed reasonable to me, my husband found it unacceptable. "Your female prejudice is showing," he said. Well, maybe.

Because of this, I will go only so far as to say that it is sometimes harder for grandfathers to relate to grandchildren than for grandmothers. Some people, too, relate to particular ages of grandchildren more comfortably than to other ages. Some of us are Awkwards only with teenagers or only with toddlers, for example.

Remember Ralph, of the Trudy and Ralph couple of Eager Beavers? Ralph is an Awkward. When Trudy went north to meet the new baby, Ralph stayed home. His future grandson was very much on his mind, but he knew it would be difficult when they got together. Ralph and his grandfather had shared many good times. They spent hours working together, hammering and sawing. He still remembers the day when they were working on the roof. "Grandfather fell off and went crashing to the ground. Everybody thought he was a goner but, after a few minutes, he got to his feet, climbed back up on the roof and said: 'I must have had a bit of a spell.'" Ralph does not do much carpentry now and doesn't know what he could share with his grandson. Maybe one day he will think more concretely about how to relate to his new grandson. Perhaps he will realize that the beach close to their retirement house is an obvious playing field, or he might make a rope swing to hang on their oak tree. For the present, however, he is an Awkward.

Grandma Ruth is a needless worrier. She lives with her husband, Mark, who works in Halifax, some fifteen miles away from their rural home. Ruth does not work outside the home. Their young married daughter, Bonny, has one child and lives not far away. Ruth worries that her daughter is too burdened with child rearing and is missing opportunities to develop other interests and further her education. She also worries that Bonny and Sam, her husband, seem unable to plan anything until they think first of the child's needs. Ruth hates to say it, but she thinks her granddaughter is being spoiled.

Ruth has forgotten that it is normal at some stages for parents to be almost totally absorbed with a new child. For all her worrying, she is unable to discuss her concerns with her daughter and is hesitant and awkward when they do talk. If her worrying could be redirected to some practical action, Ruth might overcome her inhibitions. If, for example, she were to care for her granddaughter at regular intervals, she might allow Bonny a little time for outside activities. There is nothing wrong with Ruth's concern, but it could be channeled into some useful action.

Some grandparents feel they are upstaged by their spouses. "Sarah did all the baby tending in our own household," said Sid. "How do I get into the act now with my littlest grandchildren when she takes all the initiative? She is more accustomed to the ways of babies. I feel left out because I don't know what to do. I'm really better at grandparenting when they're a little older."

Sid picked up some hints when some neighbors were discussing their grandchildren. He learned to get down on the floor with his grandbabies. Then he could watch them at eye level, see how they moved and wait for the right moment to roll a ball back.

There are no simple rules. However, if you are an Awkward looking for something better, there are two simple things you can do that will carry you a long way with most grandchildren. First, listen with attention and respect. Second, learn to play.

Play is a diversity of things. By means of play an infant learns to establish relationships with others and thus to discover her own identity. She learns about mine and yours and about sharing by accepting a toy and later moving to the excitement of passing it back and forth. Through rhythmic play, simple and repetitive, children develop strength, coordination and confidence. Play is an endless stream of necessary and meaningful activities.

An Awkward may benefit from thinking about the rhythm of play and what it means. Anyone who has reared children knows about food, sleep, diapers and fresh air. But as grandparents we have a chance to go beyond these necessities and make friends with our grandchildren.

Many adults engage in serious and disciplined games with set rules—perhaps baseball or bridge—which are quite different from the kind of play we are discussing here. Other adults have worked so hard for so many years that they have ceased to play at all. Yet anyone who rediscovers childhood play will almost automatically begin to attract children. He will also do himself a world of good by finding pleasure in the feeling of simple objects, in repetitive motions attuned to those of an infant, in experimenting with different ways of moving, in relaxing body muscles and in noticing the improved body tone that follows.

The other way to get to know children is to listen. By listening an Awkward can improve or start a relationship with a grandchild. Awkwards often go wrong in the way they try to talk to children. They tell them or instruct them, and their words fall on deaf ears. They talk down and assume the child is listening. Children turn off when the message is too long or too demanding. They have different levels of comprehension and communication than adults have.

In seminars I have given in family-life education I've asked parents to do a simple exercise several times a week: watch and record for ten minutes the conversations between adults and children, at the grocery store, on the street or at home. They discover that much of the talk is one-way, adult to child. Adults assume that the child has everything to learn from the adult and the adult nothing to learn from the child.

After a mother (it could have been a grandfather) had done some of these observation exercises she commented one day in our group: "I used to hear my three-year-old talking, soliloquizing, and I turned off. In fact, I found it annoying. Now I am tuned in and find it fascinating to hear her sorting out her world, and when I talk to her I can relate to what she really feels."

To talk with a child it is first necessary to find out what interests him. To do that you have to listen to the child. A fine adult-education teacher taught me to ask questions and then to listen to the answers. The questions you might ask could be these:

> "How come you felt so badly about that?"
> "What did it feel like to take that snake in your hands?"
> "Did you find out more about how a dam works when you visited uncle Ben's farm? Tell me about it."

Another area that can cause trouble for some Awkwards is the bestowal of gifts. Awkwards make such a big thing of it that it ruins the tone of the whole relationship with their grandchildren. When a grandchild asks: "What did you bring me today?" as soon as his grandmother arrives for a visit, you know somebody has established the wrong basis for a good grandparent relationship. It is usually the grandparent rather than the grandchild who starts this trend and, once started, it is difficult to change.

We have a close acquaintance who is perfectly aware that his grandchildren have this Pavlovian reaction to his arrival. "I don't like the tone of it," he said. "I'd appreciate it more if my grandchildren thought the most important thing I brought was me." But he finds it hard to get out of the pattern.

We are familiar enough with the grandparent who habitually slips some money to a child to go to the candy counter. Another example of overindulgence came from a step-grandmother who said, "You should see the presents we are taking to England for our grandchildren. We'll need a second plane to carry them all." In her mind a visit required parcels as concrete expressions of love. No doubt the presents evoked a good response, but there was a danger that the sheer quantity would overwhelm the more important personal aspects of the visit.

Sometimes in sheer desperation a grandparent will offer a child something prohibited. I suppose all of us have done this at one time or another, but some grandparents become hooked on such bribery. Kicking the habit is tough, but it can be done. Gifts and the giving of gifts are a normal part of grandparenting (see Chapter Ten), but in some cases they can prevent the relationship with a grandchild from achieving its full potential.

As we have suggested, there are many ways of becoming more sensitive to young children's needs. Inexperience and lack of knowledge of child development account for most of the hesitations that accompany Awkwards. They have just not spent much time paying attention to young children, and when they do, it is usually with an assumption that the child can comprehend an adult's meaning. They tend to talk *at* the child rather than *with* her. During the past fifty years the study of young children has unfolded a vast new understanding of children's emotional, social and intellectual development. That knowledge has not yet thoroughly crept in to the subculture of parents or grandparents, or even of all teachers.

Cool Cucumbers

Some people simply choose not to bother much about the grandparental relationship. Peter, a grandparent of my acquaintance, explains his choice in the following way: "We live our own lives, have our own interests. We brought up our kids. Let them bring up theirs." Peter is retired and does some consulting for his former company. He spends time at home gardening and golfing "unencumbered by grandchildren," as he says. His wife, Leah, is busy with a group of friends who enjoy bridge and golf.

Grandpa Peter visits his grandchildren only occasionally and reports that the youngest drives him nuts. He recollects the struggles he shared with his wife in bringing up their children. They had special problems with their older son, who was hyperactive. "I don't feel prepared to take on such tensions again," he says. "Our youngest grandson is the spitting image of his dad."

The basic attitude of some of these Cool Cucumbers may be warmer than it sounds. Some of them really do respect the younger generation and want not to intrude in what they perceive to be the job of the parents. Past difficulties might also have left them shy and cool. As Peter said, his problems arise from his fears. Often these fears are compounded by a reluctance to talk about personal matters.

Some Cool Cucumbers get into this condition for reasons not closely connected with the grandchild. They may live far away, or there may have been a divorce or a death or a remarriage. In all these instances the best advice is that it is never too late to change. Make a frank and overt approach to the parents and to the grandchild and make clear that you are interested in establishing a relationship and mean to work at it.

No Problems

The final category I call the No Problems, and it is a pleasure to include them. I suspect the No Problems compose the majority of grandparents whose relations with grandchildren are smooth, seamless, constructive and fun. They enjoy thoroughly satisfactory relationships with their grandchildren no matter what muddles may beset them otherwise.

I cannot do better than let one of these grandparents tell her own story without interpretation. First I should like to make clear that she has faced many problems thus far in a very full life. One major shocker she experienced was in World War Two, when she and her young son came down at sea in a flight from England to Canada. She brought up a family of five children, has lived in several countries and has coped heroically with her husband's physical disability. With respect to grandparenting, however, she emerges with No Problems.

Grandma Bronwyn writes: "We spent the summer at the seaside and during that time had five different grandchildren visit, not all at once, ranging in age from four to sixteen. I have discovered, over the years, that the way I can make us a part of our grandchildren's lives is to play with them. We can always make time to play. Ben plays board games in the winter, and in the summer we have hilarious evenings of Trivial Pursuit. We find out a lot about each other this way. They are constantly admiring Grandpa for being so clever. They expect their dads to be smart as it goes with the position of being father, but dear old Grandpa? They even enjoy finding out how knowledgeable Granny is about things they don't expect her to be even interested in—like geography and history *and* the royal family! At the seaside I swim a lot with the grandchildren and I make sure I can do at least one thing better than anyone they know. They have fun trying to place bets along the beach with anyone willing to outfloat their granny.

"When they visit us in the city it's with old playmates they stay, and not with polite strangers. Incidentally, I always play games to win! With my older grandchildren I try to do something really special with them. Jillian (who is now sixteen) and I have gone to the ballet series every winter now for six years. It's always a very special evening, and we dress up most elegantly for it. We find the intervals lovely times for talking about things that really interest her with nobody to interrupt us.

"One of my dear grandsons lives on a wee farm near Toronto, with his single-parent mother and his sister. Cherished memories of mine are of listening to him in the dusk when he checks on the chickens and chats to me about their different personalities as he holds warm new-laid eggs in his square little hands. Or, being *very* careful of me, he teaches me to climb the tree. And *I* help *him* bring in the wood and he learns that grannies are fun but can't carry much of a load. He feels strong and certain as he walks beside me. I paint pictures with my fourteen-year-old granddaughter and we drink tea and eat cookies, which she bakes."

I shall not try to explain how to become a No Problem grandparent. In my own experience as a teacher, a parent and a grandparent, I have lots of problems. It is because of the problems that I was moved to write this book. Perhaps learning to cope with your problems and, even more, occasionally succeeding in helping someone else is, in fact, the secret to being a No Problem grandparent.

3

Ages and Stages

Grandparents have been through it before, but it is useful to remind ourselves of the behavioral changes to be expected in children of different ages. We greet the newborn as a miracle, we engross ourselves in the preschoolers and we sense the sea changes beginning to take place in the "over sixes." But when we are closely involved, we don't always notice the changes. It helps sometimes to stand back and remind ourselves of the highlights and peculiarities of growth in young children.

Progress is not smooth. Equilibrium succeeds disequilibrium in the human growth cycle with periods of security and insecurity, boldness and shyness, initiative and reflection. Not all children develop at the same rate, but they tend to reach certain milestones in approximately the same order.

Expecting

The first news of the anticipated birth may alarm or thrill, depending on expectations and situations. A teenage pregnancy can stun grandparents, not to mention the parents. An unwanted pregnancy elicits negative reactions, commiseration and, because we come from an earlier generation, embarrassment. Whatever your attitude toward abortion, adoption or keeping a child in the family, a pregnant teenager needs some professional counseling, and you should encourage her to find it. There is a lot of experience to draw on, and advice is best sought as early in the pregnancy as possible.

A planned and desired pregnancy is a delight to the whole family. Parents-to-be, of course, worry about the responsibility and may want to talk to the grandparents-to-be about their doubts and worries. One major question is money. The mother may have to give up her job for a few months or longer. If maternity leave is not available at her place of work, the loss of income will be a big concern to the family. The cost of equipment for baby can be large or small, depending on the circumstances. Living costs mount; even diapers are a big expense. Grandparents who can help out financially at this stage are usually happy to do so. If they are at a low level of financial security themselves, it will be harder to contribute. (See Chapter Ten.) But there are other ways to lend support.

Prenatal

During the prenatal period, questions constantly occur to the expectant mother. Should she go to prenatal classes? How important is exercise? Grandparents-to-be are wise to encourage prenatal programs that include preparation for childbirth and baby care. Postnatal classes are also recommended. Other questions are worth discussing. What should she eat? Throw away junk food; say hello to skim milk, leafy greens, fruit, whole-wheat and oat bread, eggs, fish and liver. What about breast-feeding? Babies get protection against many illnesses by being nursed. Breast milk is inexpensive and available, and nursing is a natural security-builder for baby (and for mother). Will the arrival of a baby involve major changes? Yes. Grandparents know it is a time of family adjustments. They can make their experience available, but they had better not be pushy about it. The parents-to-be will soon learn for themselves.

Some grandparents-to-be are not far away from parenting themselves, or are even still at it. They may feel trapped by the arrival of a grandchild. Here is more responsibility just when they thought freedom was around the corner. With luck, resentment will fade once the baby is born. In fact, it may disappear the minute they are together.

Baby

Be there, if you can

Grandparents who help with newborn grandbabies feel very close to them. A friend of mine expressed it this way: "My mothering instincts explode and I can do no other than rush in to help." To hold the newborn baby in your arms is to experience ecstasy. The reflections you have at that time about your past and the future are melded into one unit—your family.

Mother and new baby require special attention. Baby's healthy development depends to a large extent on Mother's postnatal health. Grandparents' contributions at this time are usually warmly appreciated. But a word of caution: Don't take over the mother's role. Some grandparents, in their enthusiasm, leap in to care for the baby leaving Mother, in her weary state, with all the chores. Mother can be jealous. This may not be the kind of help she had in mind, although she is delighted to share some baby time with loving grandparents.

Even if you live a long distance away, consider visiting for the first week or so (that is, if the new mom and dad agree). You can help with shopping, nursery needs, preparing and freezing special dishes. Some grandparents even make things like a cradle, table and shelves, hollow blocks, sandbox, slide or fence.

One important role a grandparent can play is to give the parents some time to themselves and the mother an opportunity for rest. The husband, at this time, may be feeling a bit isolated and in need of some special attention. Even good babies require frequent feedings, and most new parents are constantly tired.

If baby is colicky and cries a great deal, the parents may be at their wit's end. They may even feel they are failures as parents. Fortunately the holding and rocking of baby gives the mother a sense of warmth and support, too. Mother-baby bonding is a crucial factor at this stage of development. It is a relief, however, to have a grandparent share some of the strains and satisfactions. There is more understanding today of the causes of colic. The problem need not be a lingering one. If the grandparent can take the baby for an hour or so, the mother can have a much-needed rest and be better able to give appropriate care to the baby.

Baby's gradual awareness of life develops through feeding, tending, caressing and stimulating. Baby's dominant needs are for nourishment, affection and trust. Trust gradually extends beyond Mother to include family members and other people. A young child's feeling of security is dependent on her perception of being protected and loved.

The sooner grandparents cuddle baby, rock her, talk to her, feed her, the sooner communication is developed. Communication with babies cannot be achieved by remote control, only by a touching relationship. Grandparents, along with other family members, can help provide some of the security baby needs, and the comfortable feelings she develops toward the outside world. If there is a good relationship with our children and their spouses, and if we are genuinely fond of babies, we grandparents can assist in many ways.

Don't overstimulate or overanticipate

Playing with baby, stimulating his curiosity by moving objects into his vision, grasping fingers and making eye contact are important ways of getting to know your grandchild. Overstimulation (sudden movement, loud noise, hot or cold shocks) is unwelcome and unfair to baby.

Grandparents, in all innocence, also make the mistake of labeling a child's personality before he's a few months old. "He looks just like his uncle. I know he'll be a bright one." "He's fussy, just like my first. He'll be a sensitive kid." "Strong — is he strong!—a future football player, just like his dad." Such predictions can irritate parents and may even open some old wounds. They also unfairly categorize the child, who cannot even walk yet, let alone defend himself.

Developmental charts

Grandparents and parents sometimes expect their baby to beat the pace of normal development. Awareness of the stages helps us to respond with good judgment. For example, we won't expect her to hold her head up much before three months or sit up without wobbling before seven or eight months. At nine months (more or less) she will be crawling, possibly backward. At ten months or sooner, she will try to pull herself up. At eleven or twelve months she may start to walk with help. Accepting these growth changes with a flexible attitude makes for a more comfortable approach.

Pushing baby toward these goals will not help, but giving him space, opportunity and loving attention will bring out his potential. Grandma Helen claims she began to appreciate the pace of her granddaughter's development at a grandmothers' group. "Just seeing the other babies, some more advanced and some less advanced, and hearing the leader of our group talk about the great strides babies make after their first year gave me encouragement. The leader put development in perspective for me and reminded me of the spurts of growth to come."

Shyness, which all babies display from time to time, is not necessarily a character trait, but a new stage of awareness of others and a need to withdraw for a bit before moving ahead. Grandparents sometimes feel hurt if baby doesn't come to them freely. We need to be aware of occasional genuine problems of separating from the mother or care giver. According to experts, around eighteen months is the height of separation anxiety, although it can start as early as nine months. It continues to recur, but lessens with the use of language.

Toddler and Preschooler

Eighteen months to two years

Our baby is now on the go, on a one-way street—his way. At this time he needs constant watching and physical limitations to keep him from hurting himself. A toddler's mobility is his greatest asset. He can now move with greater freedom to explore his environment. To the baby, no means go. "Come here" means "Go in the opposite direction"; "bye-bye" may bring him to you. He has so many abilities he hasn't mastered, he can't wait. Now is the only time he knows.

No is a part of his learning program and can be accepted by him if we are not too emotionally upset by his self-willed out-of-bounds adventures. Endless exploration and practice of motor skills can at times exhaust even the strongest grandparents. Even a walk around the block can take more time and energy than you think it will.

Safety Through physical movement a toddler learns self-confidence. She is inquiring into space and objects and functions. Walking backward, running, jumping, pushing, pulling and climbing can become defiant actions that test the patience of grandparents. From *her* point of view she is developing initiative and needs some leeway to become as independent as possible.

Safety is essential, especially at grandparents' house, which is usually adult- rather than child-oriented. Grandparents should try to see the world from granddaughter's point of view. She needs a few routes marked—possibly a gate at the top of the stairs and areas to explore that are free of breakables and dangerous wires. Other safety factors for grandparents to check are:

Keep matches out of reach.
Replace frayed electrical cords and cover plugs with adhesive tape.
Put cords for kettles, etcetera, out of reach.
Have secure screens for fireplaces.
Turn spouts and handles away from easy reach.
Windows and exit doors should be safely closed.
Pills, medicines, plastic bags, knives, scissors, pins, razor blades and so on should be kept out of reach.
Crib, high chair and car seats should have safety harnesses.
Adults should be with children whenever they are near or in the water.
Outdoor fencing should be checked.

A two-year-old does not respond well to verbal direction. You need to pick him up and redirect him instead of calling to him, and it is wise to arrange his environment with lots of opportunity for physical play. Beneath this superactive child there is a confident little person becoming more stable. He is surer on his feet. He watches people and is more affectionate. This is a short period of equilibrium. Watch out—he is on his way to becoming a Terrible Two.

The Terrible Twos

Somewhere around two-and-a-half, our dear grandchild becomes contrary again. She is trying out her newfound powers. Her "go" signs are strong, and her "stop" signs weak. Her emotions are high. She is motor minded; needs to push and pull, load and unload, haul, climb and jump, pile things up and push them down. Her feelings are both positive and negative. She still trusts you to protect her, and needs lots of support, cuddling and diversion with simple explanations.

Some grandparents, not understanding a small child's comprehension of time, may threaten to punish him later if he repeats a negative activity. Problems should be handled on the spot, not delayed to a time when reasoning may not seem relevant to the child. I asked my eight-year-old granddaughter one day: "How do you think we can help active Frankie [age two-and-a-half]?" Jane said, without hesitation: "To get him away from doing bad things you have to give him fun toys." Not bad advice for grandparents.

Toilet training Toilet training is our young preschooler's biggest challenge and is best guided by the parents. Grandparents should follow the parents' suggestions on this subject. The task may begin around two or before, but if toilet training is a battle, a child may develop resentment against those who force him to conform. If he is lovingly supported in this learning, he will feel good about himself, full of accomplishment and confidence. Don't expect successful training too quickly. He will have relapses occasionally, especially at his grandparents' house.

Comfort needs A small child has a tremendous need for comfort throughout these stages of growth. An old baby blanket (with the satin edge worn thin), a rag doll or bunny may be all-important. She may need these comforts even more when she is staying with you, the grandparents. She is hanging on to her "safety blanket." Remember: separation anxiety is high at this age. Don't criticize her special security props.

Language and communication Language and communication grow through continuous dialogue, naming, practising sounds, singing and babbling. Using his vocabulary, listening to it and adding to it, identifying objects that he focuses on in a store or in your house are parts of vital communication. By eighteen months a child may say "bye-bye" and "Mommy come." He may identify objects by name and say no a lot to express his needs. He may even say no when he means yes just because he can say it. By two years he will know many words, and by three he will talk constantly.

Taking time to talk to inquisitive children is very rewarding. When reading to them, let them interrupt. Let them "read" to you. Grandma Sarra describes how her three-year-old granddaughter holds the book open facing Grandma and "reads" the story the way her teacher reads to her in nursery school. She knows the story so well that she can repeat it easily. Parents and grandparents can play a big part in encouraging reading skills.

Social graces A child's social skills often fall short of a grandparent's expectation. Patience! Two to three is the age of a new self-confidence and experimentation and sometimes temper tantrums, of saying no more often than yes. Arguing doesn't help. Letting him stomp it out is often the best solution. Then he gets to know stomping is not an effective way to get what he wants.

Three

This is a stage of self-awareness, of wanting to help, of listening to stories (and asking for familiar ones) and of cooperation. It is a stage of equilibrium. The three-year-old likes rituals. She runs and somersaults and manages well the routines of dressing, using the toilet and sleeping. She is becoming aware of her separateness as a person. She is getting a little sense of her own worth and responsibility. But at the same time she is also at a stage of reflection and fears. Bed-wetting, for example, often recurs around this age. Accept it as an accident. Sometimes stuttering begins around three. Specific attention to the problem makes it worse. Confidence-building and good communication are the best answers, and grandparents can be a help with both.

Threes make great companions for grandparents. They like to please and they like to go places with you and do what you do. They are not "agin the government" as much as twos and fours are.

Grandma Carol was walking in the woods with her three-year-old granddaughter, Rose. They were both busy collecting things. Rose was focusing on smooth round stones, which she rubbed against her face and licked with enjoyment. She looked up at Carol and said: "What's collecting, Granny?" Collecting things was a normal grandmother-granddaughter activity for them, one that Carol, a naturalist, thoroughly enjoyed promoting. Rose adopted her grandmother's proclivity. Carol says last winter Rose had the biggest collection of icicles in Kingsmere. A typical three, Rose likes following a pattern set by Grandma.

Four

This age is more daring. Four-year-olds require a watchful eye on the part of parents and grandparents and considerably more attention to their play needs. Motor skills improve in this year, although usually social graces do not. Verbally, the four often challenges the adult. One evening when Grandma Jean was giving the children their bath, she noticed that Georgia, four-and-a-half, was scratching her neck. Jean asked her if something was wrong. Although Georgia said there wasn't, Jean persisted: "You are doing so much scratching. Is your neck itchy?" Georgia's response: "There's no law against scratching, is there?" Instead of labeling such a remark rude, it is best to realize that Georgia was trying out her rights and verbal skills.

Four-year-olds frequently test limits and try out their physical powers. They are often verbally defiant, boastful and brashly confident. Since he is reaching out for more independence and self-importance, a four-year-old cannot, at the same time, be as compliant as a three-year-old. His physical growth is rapid, outstripping his emotions, giving an impression that he is out of control sometimes.

Grandparents should remember that he is not just a more competent three-year-old. He is restless to be up and learning. He finds sit-down activity less attractive than he did at three. Excursions with opportunities to explore are high on his list of activities to do with grandparents; and as you wander through the shopping mall with your four-year-old, it is quite likely that he will scoot off and disappear for a while to frighten you. If you don't mind the expense, you might divert your four-year-old grandchild with a video game when he gets bored with shopping.

Fours like discussion and argument. Inquiry is their middle name, physical inquiry when possible but also a lot of thinking out loud, as we see in the story of Georgia. Once she said to her grandfather: "I know God made everything, but what I want to know is where did He get all that stuff?"

Four-year-olds like to be read to, but be prepared for interruptions and inquiry. Lengthy grandparent talk can quickly be cut off, as in the case of telephone conversations when grandparents go on too long. Grandma Rachel received a long-distance call from her four-year-old granddaughter on Easter Sunday morning when she was away on a holiday. After what Rachel thought was an enthusiastic response on her part, but one that obviously went on a bit long, her granddaughter said: "Happy Easter, Grandma and Grandpa. Bye now, I have to eat my Easter egg."

Five

At five, children are again easier to live with, helpful and more relaxed. Their needs may include more intellectual as well as physical stimulation. Socially, a five-year-old is often A+. Sometimes acting older than he is, he tries very hard to do what is expected of him, although he still has some doubts and hesitations.

As his grandmother was about to turn his light out for the

night, Roger looked up at her and said: "I'm not afraid of the dark, I'm allergic to it." His intellect was showing through his emotions.

When our five-year-old grandchildren are cooperative for an hour or more, we tend to think they are capable of maintaining this standard. This is a mistake, and pressure on them can result in some unfortunate habits: nail biting, nose picking, nervous coughing or a return to thumb sucking or stuttering. Don't expect them to grow up too quickly. Five-year-olds are at an attractive stage of equilibrium, ready to listen and play with others, to experiment with a variety of media, but along with their rapid intellectual development they need lots of big muscle play to work out their tensions.

Play

Play is a key ingredient in a child's development. Grandparents can enrich their grandchild's understanding of life or dull it by how they respond to and participate in her play. Don't just put a child out to play. Watch, participate occasionally and provide for meaningful play. A review of play from the baby stage through the preschool years may remind us how our grandchildren's play interests reflect their growth needs.

Baby, with her plastic cups, pots and pans and wooden spoons, is finding out how things fit, the noises they make, the power she has. Some grandparents think they need to provide a duplicate of toys that their grandchild has at home, but that is not necessary. Indoors, the bathtub or sink, under Grandma's supervision, is an ideal spot for play. We can provide play materials of ordinary everyday items. With a safe play space and some participation from a loving grandparent, a grandchild can learn about the world and the feelings of those close to her.

You might want to purchase some play materials for your grandchild that will attract him to creative play. Here are a few suggestions.

crayons—thicker ones for younger children
newsprint paper, in large sheets for painting
 paints that you mix yourself, with thick brushes, not
 paint boxes with little thin brushes
cars and trucks, especially dump trucks
a doll or two
books, as many as you can get from the library
old magazines to cut up

Young children enjoy playing house—"You be the mommy and I'll be the little boy." These games often reflect the problems and solutions to their own household situations. Social play is a child's way of finding out how people relate to each other. A supply of old hats and scarves, skirts with elastic tops to pull on, shoes and other household items such as boxes and plastic jars are all suitable play materials.

Play for older preschoolers involves lots of running, galloping, shouting and play fighting. Although grandparents may prefer to watch these activities, they can also help or teach their grandchildren some physical skills: throwing a ball, bicycling and swimming, for example.

Discipline

In my interviews, discipline was often mentioned as a major concern of grandparents. Some felt the children were allowed far too much freedom at home, and they wanted permission to take a firmer hand when they were in charge. Others, interestingly, took the reverse position. "Those kids of ours are hard on their children. Because they both work in a competitive world, they expect their poor children to work and behave like little grown-ups. Their expectations are too high."

Seventy-five-year-old Grandma Hertha remarked, in the presence of her husband: "I'm a strict disciplinarian." Her eighty-year-old husband, Herman, piped up: "I spoil 'em rotten." Once that was off their chests we talked about how they really did it. "Oh, of course you have to have rules for their safety," said Herman. "I think I'm kind to them even when I insist on rules," said Hertha. Each of them was reaching for an explanation of why their theories worked. In fact they both used the prime ingredient of good discipline—respect for the child.

Discipline for the very young child

Most grandparents say that discipline is not a major problem with babies and toddlers, but the truth is, our attitude toward discipline with young children matters a great deal. And the clue to it hangs on a very fragile but all-important issue—that of treating children as people.

A young child's earliest natural expressions involve a lot of crying, whining and rambunctiousness. These very expressions, full of meaning to him, often drive adults crazy. They seem not to understand that the child cannot help himself; that these feelings are part of being a child along with all his attractive expressions, like gooing and cooing, smiling, hugging and sleeping. I once had a neighbor whose baby cried a great deal. This mother was alone without the support of a husband. In desperation she spanked the baby for crying. She did not know how to help him or how to seek advice. Some grandparents, in their effort to control a whining or rambunctious grandchild, use physical force without hesitation.

Slapping and spanking are, however, unproductive and unsuited to learning. They undermine mutual trust and lead to feelings of hostility or open rebellion. Threats of spanking also poison relationships. The key is respect. Half the battle of discipline with babies and toddlers can be won by substituting an attractive activity for one that is leading to disaster. Emphasize the positive.

If parents and grandparents fail to treat a young child's feelings with understanding and respect in the early stages of her growing up, they will probably not understand her strong feelings, both positive and negative, at later stages of development. Children tend to behave as children. If a child pushes another child, grabs a toy or bites, it does not seem bad to him. He is doing what comes naturally. He wants the toy. Instead of pouncing on him or saying, "Give that truck back to Bobby this very minute," try speaking to him about the problem. "It hurts Bobby when you bite him; he doesn't like it," or, "Bobby is playing with that truck. He needs it for a little longer, and then it can be your turn." At the same time, redirect him to another toy.

Similarly there are positive and negative ways to handle necessary chores. Grandpa could say: "We will be having lunch soon. In a few minutes I will ask you to put your toys away," *not*, "Hurry up and clean up this mess." Or he could say, "These blocks need to be put away so we can have room to walk," *not*, "You get to work and put these blocks where they belong."

Set the stage With preschool children whose main game is locomotion, it is crucial to plan a play space so that you are not constantly saying no to their ideas. Remove as many breakables as possible. Clear wires, valuable papers, tippable chairs, lamps and plants. Picture the route of a preschool child intent on crawling up on furniture and over obstacles and pulling open drawers. Close off areas that are dangerous by shutting doors. Set aside a drawer or cupboard with materials your grandchildren like—a box of poker chips or a bag of scrap materials, for example.

No-no's The precious possessions children must not touch should be clear no-no's. A hurtful action such as throwing sand in someone's face is also a no-no. Provide an explanation and redirection. Holding a child as you explain a no-no is a better method than shouting at him. Thinking about how we grandparents feel when we are tired, bored, fearful or hungry might help us understand a small child's negative behavior and prevent us, perhaps, from reacting emotionally.

If you are taking your grandchildren for a long ride in the car, take a bagful of toys and a few snacks. Make it clear that there should be no fighting because you cannot drive safely if they fight. Elicit their suggestions about how to avoid fights.

Take their hints: perhaps a toy for each one would help, or let one sit in the front seat on the way to the ice-cream store.

Temper tantrums What about tantrums? According to some authorities, tantrums are best left alone. If you react emotionally, you can be assured of a repeat performance in the future. The theory is that if tantrums aren't rewarded, they will be shorter lived, and the lesson you want taught will be achieved: that tantrums don't ultimately work as a way to get what you want.

Grandparents' overreaction to temper tantrums is sometimes an expression of their own repressed anger. You may have held in your feelings when you were growing up in order to please a parent, and you may find an outlet in being angry with your grandchild. If you react by spanking, you will only heighten the drama. Sending a child to his room when you are annoyed with him may provoke him to greater heights—banging or breaking things. And don't try to reason with a child in the middle of a tantrum. You can't get through to him.

If your grandchild is too disruptive or hard on herself, try holding her calmly and objectively. Tell her you understand her anger and you want to help her. This method says you care about her enough to keep her from hurting herself and other people. Firm holding with a loving attitude tells her you are on her side and will help her control herself.

Time-out Children four years old and up can often be helped to behave more acceptably by calmly having them go into another room for a short while. Tell them to come back when they are ready to play without hurting anyone. If the hurting goes on, send the child away again. This can be done without anger. It is just a pause that refreshes. "It's Grandma's way of stopping us fighting," said one child, "and that's really okay." If there are several children, separating them for a while sometimes slows the tempo, stops the quarreling and lets peace reign for a bit. Another four-year-old says: "You can't fight when there's only one."

A note from Fred Fred writes from Washington about discipline: "When I was growing up the parental and grandparental approach was the oft-heard phrase, 'Children should be seen but not heard.' Fortunately the present attitude has made a 180-degree turn. Self-expression is now encouraged. Frequently too much self-expression or some other behavioral manifestation is nothing more than a reflection of frustration or a need for attention.

"The grandparent, like the parent, must recognize that a bright, healthy child is filled with ideas and imagination and frequently seeks center stage. Sometimes these characteristics present difficulties for the grandparents as well as the parents. Measured discipline is vital but *never* should be that great as to break the child's spirit. To the extent that the parents' approach in these matters raises questions in the minds of the grandparents, the grandparents should tactfully discuss the matter with them."

Good advice, Fred.

4

Ages and Stages Continued

Middle Childhood

Middle childhood—from age six to eleven—is a steadier period, on the whole, with fewer ups and downs than the preschool stage. The six-year-old is an exception to this general picture.

Six

The six-year-old is usually in her first year of going to school all day. From her point of view, school is a strongly competitive atmosphere. She is forced to measure up to classmates, and her life is structured by timetables. She must also endure a long day away from home. She is actively pursuing interests in all directions at once and often lacks concentration. She may find focusing on school tasks very difficult and may escape into the imaginary world of daydreams. Grade One is a tough year to teach, teachers say, but the good teacher understands the daydreamer.

We grandparents could take a tip from her. "When you're finished looking at the stars, Susan, perhaps you could answer my question." Or: "Would you like a little time to tell us a story? We could wait a few minutes for you to do that, before we go on with our reading." Labeling her a daydreamer or scolding her for woolgathering doesn't help.

Our six-year-old is now more on her own. She is expected to accept a full day's program at school, but needs a warm reception when she gets home. She needs to know who will be there. If Grandma is looking after her for the day, then Grandma needs to be clued in on where she can play, who her playmates are and what to encourage. Grandma will, of course, have a snack ready. If our six-year-old has younger siblings at home, she may ask about what she missed out on by being away at school all day.

From six to eight is a time of tremendous physical activity, but grandparents do not need to organize games. A simple game of catch can satisfy most kids. Leave the more complicated games to school or Brownies and Scouts. And don't do things with your grandchild that you don't enjoy. He will know, and that will spoil the fun.

Sixes are often very thoughtful in a confused sort of way. Elaine describes some delightful sayings of grandson Donald (who was going through some puzzling thoughts about his parents' recent divorce).

"I suppose my mommy was adopted."

"No, Donald, she wasn't."

"But, Grandma, she must have been because I've never seen you big and fat in front."

It turned out that a friend of his mother's looked that way, and it was explained to Donald that it was a sign of a baby. He has found the tangled relations in the separated family a little confusing. Recently I asked him, "Where's Harry?" and he said solemnly after some thought, "If you are looking for the father of my mother, he's in the living room."

Seven and Eight

Sevens are more malleable. Their confidence grows, especially if it is supported by teachers, parents and grandparents who recognize individual qualities and don't make competition a weapon.

Teasing at school is sometimes a harsh reality. Grandparents can help most with this problem by sensing an uncomfortable feeling in a troubled story your grandchild may tell you. Lend your support, sympathize and express your confidence in his ability to cope. Finding the balance between protecting or rescuing your grandchild and trusting his ability to handle the situation is important.

Seven- and eight-year-olds often enjoy bringing friends home for supper and for sleep overs. Grandparents can take advantage of this interest to encourage the occasional sleep over with a friend at the grandparents' house. Children of this age enjoy special family excursions. Meme's granddaughter Casey, age eight, said: "I have the greatest time when Meme takes me with her to visit her other grandchildren. They're my cousins, you know, and do we have fun!"

From age six to age eleven, the child is faced with big tasks. He must master his schoolwork. He must compete in sports and try his hand at many other extracurricular activities. His interpersonal relationships take effort, and he feels miserable when he is out of sorts with his peers. He has big assignments, and they can feel even more demanding than they are. Grandparents can help in many subtle ways to relax his pressures.

Games

Playing card games or table games with your grandchild is a fun way to build his confidence and his mathematical skills. Other games that are tops in the middle years include I spy, twenty questions, charades and many more. There are some new games in the stores, called Cooperation games, which are quite popular with some grandparents, for example "Going to Granny's House," "Harvest" and "Sleeping Grump." And then there are the latest fads, like Mutant Ninja Turtles, which the young seem to delight in, though just why defeats me.

When you are choosing games, your intuition will often provide a more dependable guide than the age-level labels on the boxes. And don't forget that your grandchild's parents know their children's preferences for games.

The freer and more imaginative forms of grandparent-grandchild play such as skipping stones in the water, collecting things, swimming, playing catch and even running together are popular activities.

When I asked my eight-year-old granddaughter about what she liked to do with grandparents she said, "I like swimming, going on beach walks, picking beans and cherries in their garden. I like it when they teach you new things like cut-out puppets and when they take you to the zoo or to the movies."

Your grandchild may be a natural in sports. But at this age sports injuries are frequent. If he is on a highly competitive team and faces being laid off by injuries, he may need a good deal of support. (The American Academy of Pediatrics has stated that competitive sports should not begin until a child is twelve or older.) Even if your grandchild is a hockey or baseball or swimming star, it is wise to encourage other interests as well, such as painting, drama, camping, carpentry, music and cooking—things you can share with him.

If she is only modestly interested in sports, don't ask constantly: "How are you doing in baseball?" Find out what some of her real interests are, and encourage those. One grandfather staked his granddaughter to a course in cartooning. She's on her way to becoming the school poster maker and is thrilled with her ability.

Reading is a marvelous activity, but schools too often unintentionally discourage children by requiring specific reading assignments. Taking a grandchild to a bookstore or a library and letting him choose his own book is usually a hit, even if the book is a comic book. Reading aloud may be old-fashioned, but it is a lovely way to encourage interest in books.

Nine to Eleven

At ages nine to eleven children often group together in gangs of two or more close friends. The whole point of these gangs is that they are self-directed, not adult-directed. They are usually out-of-school groups, often neighborhood based, and they are a new reference for ideas and behavior. They are important, venturesome and private. Don't be disappointed, therefore, if your grandchild prefers going to the store with the gang to playing a game with Grandpa.

Grandma Fran thought her ten-year-old granddaughter Anne should spend more time after school with her cousin Becca, age eight, who lives around the corner. Anne, however, wanted to get away from Becca, and she needed time with her school friends. She was not expressing disrespect for Grandma or for Becca. Identification with her peers was important to her and a necessary part of her development into a self-directed adult.

In their desire to be part of the gang, preadolescents often seem irresponsible. To explain his tardiness, eleven-year-old Sandy told his grandmother, "When I told you I'd be home at nine o'clock I didn't realize my friends were going to have a marshmallow roast. I just couldn't leave then. In fact, I kind of forgot the time." This kind of behavior, annoying as it is, is normal for an eleven-year-old.

For the child of the middle years, the family is still of major importance. Her other worlds of school and the gang are strong influences, and she may often defy the parents' and grandparents' suggestions in order to test some new ground, but she is still deeply attached to parents and grandparents. Their kitchens, their picnics, their conversations and their affection for the child are her staff of life.

> Dear Grandma and Pop Pop:
> Camp is going grate. I have a grate cabin and the riding is fun. Tomorrow our cabin is going on a four day horse back trip. The trip will be real fun. I miss you, and hope to see you soon. I can hardly wait to go on this trip.
>
> Love,
>
> Theo

> Dear Gram,
> Sorry uncle Ted died. Hope you are having a wonderful time.
>
> Love,
>
> John (age twelve)

As grandparent, you serve as one of your grandchild's role models. You may not find this easy to believe at the time, because she is unlikely to be much impressed by your clothes (out-of-date) and the way you comb your hair (not with it). But wittingly or unwittingly, you have an influence on him, with your value system, your sense of humor and your ways of doing things. And as her characteristics become more clearly defined during this period, so do her aspirations for the future.

Preadolescent

The preadolescent stage (eleven to thirteen) is similar to the terrible twos and the frustrating fours. Like those stages it is a prelude to a new organization of the child's personality. It is not, however, the most popular age for parents and grandparents.

The preadolescent seems to react negatively to everything. We grandparents should avoid taking these negative reactions personally. Keep in mind that unbecoming behavior is normal at this age. Decide what is important and what is unimportant. Look beneath behavior that bothers you. Your grandchild won't want to talk to you if you constantly scold her or give her a hard time. Instead, give her a chance to air her feelings and let you know about them.

The struggle to grow up takes positive and negative forms. Grandparents applaud when children learn to walk, to talk and to count, to read, to write and to make friends, but we have a harder time when they are stubborn, defiant and indifferent to things we think are important. Expressions of independence and competence can seem negative. We grandparents have been through it before with our own children, so we should be able to keep some perspective on developmental stages. It might help to recall that underneath rebellion lurks curiosity, a sense of adventure and an eagerness to try new things.

Preadolescent eagerness sometimes makes our grandchildren forget promises and plans. Their contrary behavior is normal and temporary. If we can look below the surface of these expressions and try, in a nonjudgmental way, to understand what they mean, we will be miles ahead, and quite probably have made a good friend.

Humor is an asset in coping with certain irritating habits. In her book, *When Your Child Drives You Crazy*, Eda LeShan remarks: "When Ronnie comes home mimicking his tough pals by answering our requests with 'So what? You can't make me' 'You wanna bet?' and other more unprintable declarations of emancipation, we can get huffy and stern, moralize and punish—*or* we can joke about it. 'Boy are we getting tough!' said with a wry smile....This carries as much of a message as a lot of parental or grandparental sermons — perhaps more."

Discipline

Sometimes it's important for kids to know that, as grandparents, we have different rules and expectations than their parents do. Grandma Babs was in the kitchen during a visit from her young family and came out to find her grandchildren tap dancing on the dining-room table. The parents were paying no attention. When she told them to get down, they replied that at home this behavior was fine. In the presence of her adult children this grandmother was able to say that she had no trouble with their rules in their home but that at Grannie's house the rules are different. Grannie set a clear limit, and was, at the same time, respectful of her adult children's right to make their own decisions in their own home.

Grandma Maria complains that her grandchildren don't respond well to her when she asks them to fetch things from the store or do special chores. Her grandchildren say: "Grandma has no interest in what *we* do. She doesn't play with us or talk to us, so why should we jump to her tune when she asks us to do things for her?" Grandma Maria is interested but she is shy, doesn't speak English and avoids initiating discussions. It becomes a vicious circle with unfulfilled expectations on both sides. Discipline then becomes negative and loses the strength of good guidance.

Giving in to the temptation to look the other way when confronting serious discipline problems is a weak solution. Children need rules and guidelines that help them maintain self-control and let them know that their parents and grandparents care about them. Rules are best established in concert.

When grandparents are to be left in charge, joint parent-child-grandparent discussion about limits is called for. My interviews suggest that grandparents and grandchildren agree there should be some leniencies about such matters as bedtimes when children are with grandparents, but these don't include breaking agreed-upon rules or avoiding the responsibility for unethical behavior. If such behavior is ignored, grandchildren will not be safe in their grandparents' care.

Sometimes the lack of firm guidelines stems from a grandparent's fear of losing a grandchild's love. Grandchildren can, however, interpret overlooking rules as a sign that adults don't care. As one child said: "There is good punishment and there is bad punishment. Good punishment helps you understand." Trying to be a pal to your grandchild and letting him get away with things is not helpful. He needs and wants you to be sensibly in control.

Rudeness and swearing

Rudeness and swearing bother most of us. One grandmother says, "When our Colorado little girls came to our house, I told them that 'Oh God' every thirty minutes or so was not acceptable. Also I ruled out 'I'm pissed off' from an eight-year-old who had left her sandals at the pool."

You can set the rules at your house but not at your children's. If a grandchild's language really distresses you, a frank talk with his parents might avoid a confrontation with the child.

Lying

Children don't lie so much as they let their imaginations roam in and out of reality. After you hear a wild tale from your grandchild, you might try a reply like: "That makes a good story," which lets your grandchild know that you know she's stretching the truth, but that avoids a confrontation.

Instead of labeling a child bad for telling a fabricated story and punishing her, help her sort out wishes from reality. As a ten-year-old I once staged a false birthday at camp. I went through the ritual of the happy birthday song and the birthday cake and then collapsed in tears. An understanding counselor (substitute grandparent) helped me in a quiet talk by saying, "Your wishes ran away with you."

Children always have a reason for lying. The reason does not justify such behavior, but it must be understood before you can help your grandchild stop. Catching the reason for a serious lie, talking about it, coping with it in a tender way helps her know that you care about her and helps her evaluate her own behavior.

If lying is frequent, it is particularly important to investigate the cause. The most common causes are jealousy, rivalry, lack of attention, stress and fear of rejection or punishment.

Homework

Should skipping homework be regarded by parents and grandparents as a disciplinary problem? According to Simon, his teacher would prefer that adults not hound children about homework. Instead they should let the consequences be a responsibility of the teacher and the student. A good approach!

Following my interview with Simon, I happened to read a newspaper article that said the most commonly asked parental question in America is, "Have you done your homework today?" Responsibility for supervising homework weighs heavily on many parents who are uncertain of the role they should play in motivating their child. The article pointed out that many families today are composed of two working parents or single parents who must spend their time on survival rather than on monitoring homework. Even grandparents who may have time to help their grandchildren are finding that emotions can rise and the price is frequently tensions between them and their grandchildren. Simon and his teacher may be right. A parent or grandparent might better ask: "Are there any questions or problems about your work that you would like to discuss?"

Blatant Disobedience

Grandparents who suspect their grandchildren of stealing or cheating should consult the parents and, with their agreement, frank discussion should follow in which the facts are clearly spelled out. There is no point in handling such discussion in an accusatory fashion. It provokes a defiant attitude in the child and accomplishes little. Listening with respect to the child's point of view can be helpful in arriving at a fair decision.

We grandparents feel good when our guidelines are respected, and children are more secure knowing that they are cared for by strong and understanding people who give them a fair shake. When major disciplinary action is necessary, we should refer the matter to the parents in whose hands these rights ultimately belong.

Parents and grandparents need to continue to offer consistent limits and guidelines against which the child can test his own ideas. It is by balancing what feels right to him with what is desired by his peers and what is required and expected by his parents and grandparents that the budding adolescent begins to develop a stronger sense of his own identity.

Adolescent

Adolescence has come to be known as a time of inner turmoil, a time of preoccupation with questions such as "Who am I?" and "Where do I belong?" Adolescents are prone to idealism as well as to a sense of futility and rebellion. They also have a new drive for independence and need more freedon from adult supervision and restraint so they can explore their own ideas and those of their friends.

Privacy is especially important. During these years a child needs some secrets and some time alone. She is developing a new awareness and a new selfhood. It is entirely normal for her to be remote at one time and in close communication with you at another.

Early Adolescent

Puberty signals the onset of adolescence. It usually occurs earlier in girls than boys by at least two years. The exact years of puberty vary greatly. For our purposes, "early" adolescence will encompass the years from eleven to fifteen, "late" adolescence from sixteen to twenty-one.

One attractive aspect of early adolescence is the child's effort to converse in adult fashion among his peers. A conversation was reported by an Ottawa grandmother when she had her six grandchildren, ages thirteen to sixteen, to dinner one night. Three of them had just come from out of town. "I found, for the first time, that the conversation had a definite adult tone," she said. "They all seemed comfortable discussing handicapped people, manners, space et cetera. Goodness knows what else they talked about when they were all by themselves."

Grandparents should not be surprised to find teenagers talking about nuclear weapons and the environment. These issues have enormous implications for them. You may be able to help them understand a world that includes the threat of nuclear war, terrorism, international drug rackets, advanced scientific ideas, international world crises and third world debt, to mention a few modern problems.

Many grandparents who were fond of their grandchildren when they were young (and pliable) become disenchanted with their teenage grandchildren's life-styles. Some of their habits *are* pretty bizarre. However, if you are willing to look under the hair and crazy makeup, you will be pleased to find many bright, inquiring minds. It takes patience to develop good feelings about a teenage grandchild. But the rewards are well worth it.

Grandmother Jessie registered delight in the conversation her granddaughter became involved in at the dinner table one night. Heather, age fifteen, was a mature and thoughtful child. Jessie had a sense that Heather was feeling fine about being included in a very important family decision.

Jessie, who was divorced, had a good relationship with her only granddaughter, the child of her son and his common-law wife. Over the years Jessie and Heather shared the strengths of each other's special personalities and talked freely about family struggles. Sitting at the kitchen table with two other family members, they are having a heated discussion about their tangled problems.

Jessie, with what she thought was reasonable consideration, had expressed an opinion in favor of selling the old family house. Her two sons argued against it. Heather piped up: "Out of all this talk, there is only one person that makes any sense and that's Granny Jessie." The others thought they were getting nowhere. Young Heather had enough self-confidence to give a considered opinion. Heather thought Granny was on the side of good sense and said so! She had talked to Jessie many times about this issue and felt entrusted with adult knowledge. Her adolescence was on a positive kick that night.

Telephone Crazy

The telephone is a vital part of most teenagers' lives. The word "crazy" in this case refers to the state of mind of parents and grandparents as they overhear teenagers spending endless hours on telephones. What the teenager is doing is essential to growing up. More specifically, he is exploring and experimenting with social contacts to find out what works and what doesn't. It is well to remind ourselves that, from his point of view, he is behaving reasonably. But he should not have a monopoly on the telephone when he is at your house. (See Chapter Five.)

There may be a long period of years in which an adolescent wants to join the adult world and is not yet ready. She is searching for her identity, and her hallmark is lack of self-confidence. She may compensate for this by experimenting with aggression, or she may withdraw. Teenagers cluster, motivated in large part by their need for mutual support during this period from which, it is hoped, they will emerge as self-sufficient functioning adults. Be available to them and remain patient. You have listened to teen talk, that peculiar language consisting partly of new idioms and partly of a dialect only they can understand. There is a good reason for this: they want to be able to communicate privately, and they want to be able to separate themselves from adults.

Drugs

In our present-day world our grandchildren are going to be confronted by drugs, and some of them will go further and experiment with them. Because a growing child will make his own decisions, he must take responsibility for them. His ability to do so depends to some extent on the guidance he was given earlier. A child is well equipped if he has already learned that he alone is responsible for the consequences of what he does.

Grandparents and parents should be able to ask adolescents about their exposure to drugs and alcohol. It's important to be inquisitive rather than rushing in with lectures. Adolescents may have a tough time saying no to drugs if they see them as the only way to be accepted by the gang. Talking about this struggle may be more beneficial than scary predictions about addiction.

Grandparents have two additional roles in this area, both useful. The first arises in the earlier formative years, when children learn basic morality. It is important that they begin early to find out how successful, functioning adults live. A grandchild is deeply impressed and remembers when grandparents occasionally confide about some of the dilemmas they faced in their own lives.

The second role arises if earlier instructions and directions fail. As a grandparent you may become convinced, through conversation or other evidence, that a teenage grandchild is taking drugs. If the parents are unwilling or unable to do anything about this, it may be up to you. Many resources are available: doctors, social workers, schools, church groups and the police. Drug addiction increases with usage, and the less time lost the better. Grandparents should make every effort to get the parents to take action, but they should not hesitate to act directly if necessary. Good professional advice is available for the asking. If you feel uncertain about how to proceed, seek consultation yourself before overreacting with the adolescent —perhaps unnecessarily.

The most impressive way to educate grandchildren about tobacco, drugs and alcohol is to set a good example yourself. This may not be easy, and we do not want to pretend we are the very model of a modern major grandparent, but, if we have a problem, it might be a good time to consider working on it.

Sex

Sexual interests and experimentation are of central importance to adolescents. Children want freedom to explore and develop their relationships but, paradoxically, they do not want complete freedom and would not know what to do with it if they got it. There is an old saying that teenagers want to be on a leash, but they want it to be a long leash. This is entirely normal.

It is probably just as well that grandparents are seldom faced with the need to provide grandchildren with sex education. Even though they are familiar with sexual facts, members of the older generation are rather inhibited in talking about them. Many of us were brought up with different attitudes, and the kids tend to regard the whole thing as less mysterious. Teenage pregnancies were by no means unknown when we went to school, but now we often hear about casual copulation. Grandparents may conclude in some cases that a child's sexual education is being neglected. The first step is to have a talk about it with the parents. When grandparents are asked these questions, they should of course answer them and encourage children to behave responsibly. In this, as in everything else, they must learn that the actions they choose to take have consequences for them.

Late Adolescence

Late adolescence (sixteen to twenty-one) is a period of more sexual interest, long-term thoughts about relationships and the future in general, education, jobs and careers. Grandchildren's reluctance to discuss these issues with parents and grandparents is in part a reflection of their own doubts and in part a shortage of time. They are so busy with sports, study and relationships that they have little time left over for grandparents.

We grandparents can remain openly curious about our grandchildren's interests. To stay in touch, we might ask about movies they have seen recently or request that they play their favorite music for us (at low volume). What contacts we have with grandchildren should try to focus on the positive and not the negative scenes. We should be willing listeners and available for talk but should not feel too frustrated if they keep their distance. They may be off in their own world.

Many adolescents are working at part-time or full-time jobs.

Many are uncertain about their future careers. Vocational guidance can be of great help. Grandparents might recommend professional vocational testing, which covers intelligence, interests, aptitudes and personality. If asked, we can also offer our own advice based on our wide experience.

Grandparents take note: your grandchildren have become adults or almost adults. They are still your grandchildren, but children they are not! Respect is called for, even when you disagree. A good relationship develops if it is based on friendship, support and, of course, a sense of humor.

Those grandparents who have devoted care, thought and consideration to being grandparents usually find that their grandchildren become their friends. It means a lot to be close to a young person who is eager to bring good news and willing to impart bad news, ready to consult and occasionally just to keep in touch.

It is never too late for grandparents or grandchildren to initiate a relationship. "At the age of twenty," my daughter-in-law said, "I became interested in my grandmother, and stayed interested in her until she died." The quest for identity and family connections never ceases.

5

Grandparents' Living Arrangements

We grandparents are not as easily available to our grandchildren as grandparents were in former years. We may still be working and have less time for frequent intimate visits with our young families. We may be retired and live a long distance away or be engaged in studies or other activities. Some of us are in retirement communities or nursing homes. Our various living arrangements have sometimes made things more complicated and sometimes have created new opportunities for us. We look, in this chapter, at the different ways in which grandparents have chosen to organize their lives or in some cases have *had* to organize their lives, due to personal circumstances beyond their control. In the next chapter, we confront the other side of the equation and observe the parents' living arrangements.

Close By

Most of us envy the position of grandparents who live close by. It recalls old-time patterns of warm, supportive relations in a three-generation neighborhood setting. Perhaps you are among these lucky grandparents. We will peek at a couple of settings that seem, for the most part, positive and enviable.

An example of supportive family living close by are my friends the Burnses. They are recent immigrants from South Africa. They left behind in their native country one daughter and her family; a son and his family live in Australia. The senior Burns family has chosen to come to Canada where a married daughter, Sheila, is living with her husband and two children, not too far away from Grandma and Grandpa's apartment. Sheila teaches at the school where her children are enrolled. Her husband works for a management consulting firm. The Burns family shares much of their life together. Grandma is usually free to pick up a sick child at school while the mother continues her teaching day. The family also gets together every Friday night at the grandparents' place for Sabbath eve suppers, and recently relatives from abroad came to Canada for their grandson's bar mitzvah.

The people in this family are not so involved with caring for each other that they ignore other interests. Grandpa works in a law office and Grandma enjoys the cultural life in her new city. Living near their younger daughter's family is satisfactory in many ways. But the Burnses have had to make major adjustments. Having moved from a substantial residence in the old country, they are adjusting to more cramped living space, a colder climate and separation from extended family. It is not always easy, but the Burnses feel the closeness they share with Sheila and her family compensates them.

Ephraim is a contented grandfather who wrote to me: "Our grandchildren live only fifteen minutes away, and we see them frequently with their parents. In addition we often baby-sit for them at their house, our house, or at our cottage."

Ephraim and his wife, Polly, enjoy having their grandchildren visit. They have all worked together to build a playhouse. "We frequently have picnic lunches at the playhouse as well as occasional sleep outs with our bedrolls. We swim together in a nearby stream. We play with them all we can. We play lots of ball and hide-and-seek, although I call a halt at tag."

Ephraim, exemplifying his philosophy of doing things *with* his grandchildren, not *for* them, is thoroughly pleased with the results. He and Polly have been invited by their grandchildren to skate and to ski. Ephraim went along on the skiing trip as an observer only. It was a high point for him to have been invited by the kids. Ephraim and Polly are devoted grandparents. Such glowing accounts are all too rare.

Many other grandparents wonder why they don't enjoy happy relationships with their grandchildren. Horace and Brenda are such a couple. They live close to their grandchildren, but do not get as much satisfaction from their roles of grandparents as they think they should.

When I questioned Horace about this, he explained: "My kids think grandparents are for their convenience. They need a baby-sitter—they phone us! They think we don't mind sitting until after midnight. We do. What I'd like is to enjoy my grandchildren when I choose, not just when their parents choose that I should."

This family, although they live close together, have not worked out their communications very well. With easy physical access they could be enjoying the relationship much more.

The problem is communication; family members need a better understanding of their interrelationships, and the grandparents could take the initiative in opening the discussion. The logistical problems seem to be formidable on both sides. The grandparents are involved in their own activities, with meetings, deadlines and schedules, Grandfather in his business and Grandmother in her voluntary organizations. The parents are busy from morning to night. If the grandparents feel they are being taken advantage of they should say so and reach for an alternate plan. This is best done in such a way as to bring the parents to consider things that have probably been worrying them, as well. It is not a question of whether they want to include each other in their lives. They do. But, rather, it is a question of reordering priorities, vocations, avocations, households, children and leisure.

Far Away

Faraway grandparents are separated from their families for many reasons. As in the past, many young families leave their parents behind when they grow up. Some move to another town or city, some to another country. Another class of faraway grandparents are those who live abroad for half the year or have retired to a warmer climate. We live in a world where there is more separation of generations. Since we cannot change the facts, the question is how do we keep in touch.

Some distant grandparents throw up their hands and do nothing. Then, when they find themselves, years later, meeting their grandchildren as comparative strangers, they realize that they missed something important. Other grandparents do something to overcome distance. Their stories have a lot in common, especially the satisfactions derived from trying to make connections.

Grandparenting from a distance is nothing new. What is new is that grandparents, who used to be able to do little or nothing to try to overcome separation and distance, now have better means of communication. Airplanes exist, and they fly both ways. It does not cost as much as it once did to pick up the telephone or send a long-distance gift certificate. And children still love to receive letters addressed to them.

Grandma Meg, a long-distance grandmother, has some other warming answers. She writes, "It is impossible to break down into words the closeness Ranny and I have with our two grandchildren we have seldom seen more than twice a year—Christmas at their house, a summertime visit at ours, one child at a time. Christmas is family time and pretty well speaks for itself. Summer visits have run from four days to six weeks. The grandchildren had the choice of whether to visit and the length of the visit. (This was subject to our convenience, and we happily made it convenient!) Because we lived in a small wooded lake community, we teased that our home each year became their summer resort. Friends made during one summer eagerly awaited the grandchild's arrival the following year. We enjoyed their enjoyment of time spent with friends and never insisted that all their time be spent with us. Their visit was their vacation from responsibilities at home—and they understood that grandparents have more time to spare than do parents. Individual likes can be catered to and dislikes sidestepped. The grandchildren loved that, too, and understood it as a summer treat.

"During these summer visits we had time for games, for reading, for sharing things of the past as well as things current. We all laughed a lot—and there were serious times. There's nothing new in the method of loving, caring, sharing, enjoying, listening—to bring joy into the lives of family members from ages zero through a lifetime. Or maybe we've just been lucky? Naturally, all isn't smooth sailing during these visits, but problems solved together often make the relationship even closer."

Margaret is a grandmother who knows how to communicate with her distant grandchildren. (She has four others close by.) She corresponds with them. She writes stories and they write poems, stories and personal letters. In one letter her twelve-year-old granddaughter writes:

> What do you do
> When your best friend says, "I don't need you,"
> When they won't let you join into the fun
> When they won't even include you as one
> When you're all alone with no one to say
> I need you, Remmie, I need you today.
>
> R.

> Dear Gram,
> What would you do?
> I'm in the library, really I'm in English class but the school is too small so we don't have an English room. We are supposed to be reading but I don't want to. I'm feeling bad because Annie and Aline are really changed. I don't know why but they are both being pretty mean to me. I got the same teacher as grade four but she is always yelling at us about how we should be able to walk down the hall silently because we are in grade six, result: Headache.
>
> Aline is always in a bad mood for reasons unknown to me. She is just about always yelling and screaming and I'm caught right in the middle. The only good things in school are the two new kids. Sherron and Ann are nice.
>
> P.S. please don't put this on the fridge.

Margaret describes her granddaugher as vulnerable. She says: "I am pleased she can talk to me. Of course I phoned her right away and then wrote her a long letter and was glad to hear that by the time she got it the situation had resolved itself. I am going there next week; can't wait to see her."

Two grandparents, Sally and Ed, wrote: "We have had the privilege (and challenge) of taking care of a happy and active two-year-old for two short periods when the rest of the family was on vacation trips. Those were experiences that, after our recovery, will be among our most cherished memories. We strongly recommend that grandparents find a way to baby-sit for at least a few days regardless of time, distance and logistics. This total-immersion approach can be an unforgettable and unifying experience for sitters and sittee, who will gain a lasting and, we hope, positive impression of what grandparents are and why they exist."

My husband and I have, for some years, been distant grandparents to one set of grandchildren. We have visited them in California when we could, and they make occasional visits to us. Our son and his wife have been cooperative and involved in these plans. We telephone and write frequently. Our son sends us tapes of speeches his children have made and newspaper clippings that record their accomplishments. Therefore, when we do talk to them, we are almost up-to-date. Long-distance apart does not need to mean isolation or lack of contact.

In the Same House

Three-generation homes were a natural arrangement in the past. Interpersonal communication was taken for granted in families where everyone lived under the same roof. Today, in our mobile, fast-paced society, communication is weak; the personal pressures of three-generational communal living create problems that require mature handling to avoid outright clashes.

Grandparents have many more outside interests these days and they want to avoid being glorified baby-sitters. Both parents and children are more likely to speak their minds, to express impatience or resistance and to battle openly when they disagree. Mutually supportive behavior has declined, while desires of family members to be separate entities have risen.

The three-generation household has ceased to be the accepted model and tends rather to be regarded as a temporary expedient. It still exists, however, and may increase as married students and unemployed parents ask to return to the nest. A working couple living in a small apartment may find that a baby is on the way; both of them have jobs but they cannot afford a house. Could they live with Mom and Dad for a while? Would Mom take care of the baby? When family lives are under stress, some parents feel called upon to act as a stabilizing force, even if this means sharing their small house.

For active grandparents this kind of arrangement is a compromise. We are glad to be able to help our children but we don't like to give up our space and privacy. We hope the stay will not be long. We may be forced to hold other activities in abeyance. Difficulties will inevitably arise. A son-in-law, for example, can easily feel himself to be denigrated as someone who cannot afford to buy a house or who cannot find a job.

Conversely, some grandparents may be in need of support. A widowed grandmother or grandfather may be unable to care for a large house, or may need special care because of illness or disability. The financial situation may make it necessary for the grandparent to live with the children.

There are no right or wrong answers to the questions raised by these situations. Some families can make a go of it, and some fail. It is unrealistic to suppose that three generations will happily share the same living room every evening. We elders want some peace and quiet, and the younger family members may want loud music. If space and budget permit, it is best for the grandparents to have a separate area in the house so that all concerned are free to come and go and to live as independently as they want.

The presence of two grandparents is both a blessing and a problem. When you and the parents differ on issues of discipline, the children may wonder who is in charge, you or their parents. When grandparents feel resentments there is some danger that they will take their feelings out on the children. As grandchildren grow older they are conscious of their rights and they may struggle with grandparents about authority issues. However, it is possible for all concerned to develop mutual support. There are other adults to defend the child when problems arise, and other smiling faces to approve of deeds well done. Planned schedules and shared responsibilities are a must for things to work well.

If the family lives in the grandparents' house and relies on the grandparents' money, the grandparents may consciously or unconsciously assume power, even over the grandchildren. This can cause serious problems. Parents have the right and the responsibility to be in charge of their children. Co-parenting may sound good to the grandparents, not to the parents. The grandparents should be supporting actors rather than stars. To do otherwise is unfair to their children.

Another arrangement is common today: a divorced daughter and her children living with the widowed grandmother. Here there are only two adults, not four, to consider on issues of rights and responsibilities. This simpler combination may enable both families to enjoy a standard of living that is higher than they could afford separately. It can allow Grandmother to keep her house, and it provides her with the companionship of her daughter and her grandchildren. It also gives the daughter a degree of freedom she would not enjoy if she were living on her own. If grandmother and daughter have a good relationship, they can work out freedoms and responsibilities in acceptable ways. It helps if Grandma works part time. Parenting is then centered on the daughter. Privacy does have to be respected, however, and it does help if both adults have clearly spelled out rights and responsibilities. Given basic respect and planned schedules, such a living plan can support individuality and not crush it. I know one family whose lives are enriched by this joining.

According to most forecasts, however, multiple housing for extended families is not a major trend. Recently the Toronto *Globe and Mail*, in an article on housing, referred to "people living in smaller groups than ever before." It continued: "Where you had four or five people living in a household, now you have two or three....Families are breaking up or forming in non-traditional ways, parents are less likely to live with their adult children. There's been enormous societal change over the last twenty-five years."

The Rotating Grandmother

Mrs. Martini shuttles among three family households. Grandma Angela has little income of her own and is dependent on her three married children, all of whom are in two-working-parent families. To understand Angela, you must know two things about her. She is devoted to her family, to the point of having few other interests, and she has a low boiling point.

When Angela was a new immigrant, she lived with her only son and his family, the neediest of her offspring. She stayed with them for three years, but when her youngest daughter was expecting her first baby she asked Angela to move in with her to help for a while. Angela agreed but said she would need to slip over to her son's house occasionally, "To do some cooking for those hungry boys." The other daughter recognized a good thing when she saw it and asked her mother to come to her for a few months. Under this system Angela moves on periodically, and each of her children looks forward to her return. Angela feels that she is paying her way and is not a burden.

Angela dotes on her grandchildren, but she also has unrealistic ideas about discipline, especially in relation to school-age boys. Her daughter-in-law says: "She doesn't understand that kids can't be quiet whenever it pleases her." Angela gets annoyed after a while. When little things begin to frustrate her, she moves on to another house. She enjoys herself most at the beginning of each visit and leaves when she needs to restore her calm.

Other grandparents live part of the time with their adult children and their families. A family I know asked their lonely widowed grandmother to move in with them. Both parents work, and their children are in school all day. Instead of burdening them and herself by staying for indefinitely long periods, this grandmother and her young family have worked out a plan that makes them all happy. Grandma keeps an apartment (fortunately she can afford to) so that she can retreat to her own quarters once in a while to restock her energies. About one month out of every three, she stays with the young family. This arrangement works because she can still afford to keep her own apartment and her health remains good. The family manages with sitters when Grandma isn't with them. She is, of course, usually on call.

The Working Grandparent

It is the rare working grandparent, in the midst of a busy career, who manages to find much time for a grandchild even one day a week. Working grandparents can find there is a conflict between their desire for independence and their desire to be close and important to their grandchildren. People who have jobs need some time by themselves for rest and for recreation with friends. They are not prepared to have baby-sitting be their principal voluntary activity, yet they want to find ways to spend time with their grandchildren.

One exceptional story is that of my friend Gilda, a working grandmother who shares one day a week with her grandchildren. It is her day off work. She picks up her two grandchildren and takes them to her apartment. She does her weekly shopping with them, allowing lots of time for curiosity and conversation. "At this stage the baby is easy. I talk a lot to her, though she is only one year old. The two-and-a-half-year-old is a going concern." Gilda wonders if this routine will still be possible when they are two and a half and four. Now she is able to manage meals, a rest time and play time, and enjoys it all. "Grandma's day" is special, full of fun and thoroughly appreciated by the parents and children.

Grandparents who have a summer place in the country or at a beach can often arrange to enjoy relaxed playtime with their grandchildren during their vacations. Grandma Laura said that the water has always been the best play area for her and her grandchildren. She learned to do the crawl one winter and boasted proudly that she amazed her grandchildren when they visited her the following summer.

A question that arises is whether to have the grandchildren visit at the same time as the parents. If the children are very young it may be easier with the parents there too, especially if the grandparents are in need of some rest. But many grandparents say: "Have them alone! It's the only way to get to know them. Play with them all you can."

When longer visits do take place, as one grandmother expressed it: "I find all my maternal juices overflowing once again." There is no doubt about this grandmother's fundamental attachment. She works at a full-time job, and her weekends at the cottage in the summer are the best times for her and her grandchildren. For most of the year other people spend more time than she does with her grandchildren. She knows that she needs to reclaim her grandchildren's affection and confidence, although it will not take her long. She has learned, during the year, to take time for occasional telephone calls. She has started to exchange notes and drawings. Out of this kind of communication she can be better prepared to pick up with the children when they do get together.

The Remarried Grandparent

If you are a remarried grandparent you have undoubtedly thought a lot about your new connections and family orientations. You may live close by or far away, and you may work or not work, but the important issue for the family will be: Are you and your new spouse still interested in us?

How each of the remarried grandparents considers the other's family is crucial. If they become disconnected from their own families, it may, of course, not be intentional. They may have drifted into becoming Cool Cucumbers, although Grandma used to be an Eager Beaver. Their new marriage may seem ideal to them but may leave some of the family feeling unconnected. A parent I was speaking to recently said his dad had remarried and was living in Florida with his new wife. "I feel as if we don't exist any more. We never get a spontaneous invitation to visit them. Any communication is always initiated by me." Your children and your grandchildren do care deeply about you. They may have been remote at times because of the pressures in their own lives, but they do not want to be left out.

It may be that there are tensions over the remarriage on the part of the younger generations, or uncomfortable vibes between two parts of the family. It may help, as it does in divorce situations, to think of the fact that your grandchild is still *your* grandchild and you are still his grandfather. A grandchild may become quite jealous of the new family member. He may feel a lack of attention. It is worth trying to make relationships as comfortable as possible for the child's and the parents' sake. If you gain new grandchildren along with your new spouse, you have an added bonus. It may take some time for them to adjust, however, and they may never totally accept you as a replacement grandparent. You can still play a part in their lives, however, if you make the effort.

Grandparents as Full-time Parents

Tragedies sometimes catapult grandparents into full-time parenting. Some grandparents have wondered at first whether they were up to it and have gone ahead and done magnificent jobs. Some children raised by grandparents look back on a wonderful upbringing with appreciation for the strengths of their grandparents' characters. I know such a family in California. Both parents were killed, leaving two children. The grandparents were getting along in years, and their means were very limited. It has been hard for them but, with the help of friends and extended family, a good relationship has ensued. Incidentally, the experience appears to have done no harm to the grandparents.

Professional assistance is essential in such cases. There are community services in most cities to aid in rehabilitation. Family service associations, parent counseling centers, children's aid societies, psychiatrists, psychologists and social workers are among the available resources. Grandparents have questions: "Are we really the best people to raise these children?" "Can we do it?" "If we undertake this responsibility, what may be some of the difficulties ahead?"

The grandparents may conclude that they are not qualified for the job. One grandparent said he and his wife took the job on for two years as a trial. After a social-work therapist helped them to consider their whole situation, they realized that it was beyond them. Their health was simply not up to the strains involved. They resolved the problem by arranging for an adoption, and they continued to maintain a close relationship with their grandchildren.

Sharing care

A widowed grandmother I know faced the tragedy of her daughter-in-law's death from cancer when her baby was nine months old. Inga, a widowed grandmother, encouraged her son to continue looking after his baby. She undertook to provide the help he needed to make it possible. In the morning Daddy bathed and dressed baby Eric and had breakfast with him. Then he took Eric to Inga's, where he stayed all day. Father came to Inga's place for dinner, then took Eric to his own house for the night.

This schedule went on for a year, and Inga is forever grateful for the intimate relationship she developed with her grandson, who is now ten. After about a year, Eric's father remarried and started a new family. Later Inga remarried. She achieved a lifetime of joy by establishing a vital connection with young Eric. Her flexibility, her ability to attach but not consume, her physical and moral strength and her newfound love all pulled together to make this arrangement work.

Sometimes grandparents must step in for the good of their grandchildren to rescue them from abusive or unstable situations. We must respond directly and immediately to cases of child neglect. Even mild forms of abuse can be shocking to grandparents. If possible, the grandparents should immediately arrange for the children to have loving care. Some of us can fill this bill either through temporary adoption or a professionally guided plan that includes a lot of grandparent input.

Marion brought her two granddaughters from the United States to live with her in Canada. They had been born in Chicago, where both parents became drug addicts. Marion said: "There was no alternative. The girls had been neglected and at ages seven and eight were beginning to be involved in petty thievery. It was all going from bad to worse. After a series of consultations with social workers and child psychiatrists at a center for disturbed children, I brought them with me to Montreal, arranged for them to be enrolled in a boarding school and to come home with us for weekends and holidays. My husband is chronically ill, and we could not take the strain of having them at home on a daily basis. They are not yet doing well in school. For a while the parents couldn't have cared less, it seemed, but they have started a rehabilitation program, and I pray that the family will be reunited soon."

Ill or Disabled Grandparents

Grandparents who are not able to maintain their own houses or apartments may ask to move in with their sons or daughters. The situation occurs most often when the grandparent is alone. Where possible, some private setting within the household is desirable, giving Grandma a chance to carry on her own interests and hobbies. If the time comes when nursing care is called for, such services are available in most communities under the public health-care system.

When an elderly grandparent lives alone and his children are concerned for his well-being, they may have trouble persuading him to leave his comfortable home. This is a tough decision, for the grandparent and for the rest of the family. If home housekeeping and nursing services are available, Grandpa could stay at home, an option many older people prefer. Family members should then develop a routine of visiting Grandpa. We may think little children would be hesitant to make physical contact with a sick grandparent, but actually they are more resilient than we imagine. Seeing Grandpa through his last years can be an enriching experience of kinship.

Two of my long-standing friends, Derrick, age ninety-four, and Mona, age eighty-six, went through some hard times. Grandma Mona was very ill, in and out of hospital for two years. Her diagnosis was uncertain. Grandpa managed to care for her in an admirable way with the help of occasional community services. Neither of them wanted a nursing home. The best solution for them, they thought, was to carry on in their own house till they dropped.

Mona was beginning to function again, with occasional relapses, when Derrick fell and had to go to the hospital. Complications were brought on as he lay in bed, and his convalescence was protracted. Finally he was able to move to his son's home. After some delay Mona was able to join him there. He was clear in his thinking and psychologically in good shape. During his final days he was happy with his young family and his only grandson. They enjoyed some fine talks together, which grandson Rod will long remember. Derrick died contentedly two days before Christmas. These arrangements had worked well for him. They were rendered possible by two things: he and Mona were financially secure enough to afford them, and his son and daughter-in-law were limitlessly devoted.

Grandparents who are cared for by their children can help to make things easier for the young family. Obviously financial help is always appreciated, but so are the small additions even bedridden grandparents can make: reading to a child, telling stories and just listening. If, however, the grandparents' presence is placing too many emotional, physical and financial strains on the family, the time may come to consider the alternative of a nursing home.

In a Nursing Home

Placing Grandma or Grandpa in a nursing home raises guilt feelings and can present a major crisis to the family. Grandchildren who have felt pressures on their limited freedom and space and have expressed feelings about it may feel partly responsible for sending Grandma away. Others who may feel guilty are parents and grandchildren who live far away.

We grandparents, if we have our wits about us, can help take the burden off the younger generation by thinking and planning ahead about this issue and accepting the move if it seems right to the family. Some of us recognize the stage of infirmity we have reached and are reluctantly willing to be moved to a more secure setting, but some of us do not—or pretend we do not—feel this need. We feel we will be cut off from the outside world and from loved ones (too true in some cases), but we feel guilty if we are burdening the family.

One of my daughters-in-law recalls her friend Amelia, who learned at the age of eighty-two that she would be blind in a few years. She went from residential community to residential community, nursing home to nursing home, looking for a place she could live in when she lost her sight. This grandmother's courage allowed her to have much more control over her circumstances than she would have had if she had waited until her handicap overcame her.

Severe illnesses and ailments produce traumas beyond the medical ones, for example loss of financial support, emotional and physical breakdown, concerns about one's partner's health. Some nursing homes are very good at coping with the total health picture and help you maintain a close connection with relatives. Assistance for the ailing elderly has grown in our communities, but more help is needed in the social and health fields to allow our aging population to live with dignity. Making connections meaningful—among family, nursing-home personnel, friends—is the challenge. Sometimes, grandchildren's needs to keep in touch with grandparents are ignored (not purposely), but with a little forethought grandparents and children can be involved in the caring process even in the nursing home.

"We took our grandchildren to Indiana to see my mother and father [the children's great-grandfather]," writes Grandma Fran. "My father is in a nursing home. He can't see much, can't talk much and often doesn't know anyone. When we went in to see him the two little girls went right to his bed, leaned over and kissed him and he looked at them and actually smiled. This was only the second time the girls had seen their great-grandfather, but I was so touched at how sweet they were to him. They brushed his hair and patted him on the cheek. My mother, who is eighty-five, was greatly moved by the children's response. We talked a lot on our way home about what it used to be like for me as a little girl."

Facing Death

Nightfall comes as the natural end of the cycle of life. Children often get their first experience of death when a grandparent dies. Some people shield children from death but, in my experience, it is good to encourage children to participate as fully as they want in final leave-takings along with the rest of the family.

When my husband was a boy his maternal grandmother asked to see him when she was on her deathbed. Her final illness had been a grueling experience, and she was not very coherent. She wanted to hold his hand. She muttered something like: "One old woman following another." He thinks she was comparing her own process of dying with that of her mother at the same stage. He remembers both the close connection to his grandmother and the glimpse she gave him of the continuity of life.

Funerals establish a sense of family history in a child's mind. My paternal grandmother was old and sickly. She lived with us during the last year of her life. I went to sit by her bedside to have her brush my hair into ringlets around her swollen fingers. She died when I was five years old. That Christmas I found a life-size baby doll under the tree. It was her final present to me and the most treasured I ever remember. Her funeral with the procession of cars moving down our street is a picture still vivid in my mind.

No matter what the situation or living arrangement, grandparents can enrich the lives of their grandchildren. Overcoming the obstacles can be a challenge, but the rewards are great.

6

Parents' Living Arrangements

With our new living and working patterns, we grandparents enjoy interesting lives. The curve of enjoyment growth, however, is slightly slowed down by the other set of life patterns to which we are all vitally connected—our children's living arrangements.

The phenomenon of the family with two working parents has dramatically changed many people's life-styles. Even the mother at home is differently situated than a mother at home was in earlier years. More families are headed by single parents or by parents who have gone back to school. The use of day care has become an accepted fact of life for many families. And the family with gay parents has become more recognized.

These complex patterns and our entanglements in them can cause us difficulties in our efforts to relate to our grandchildren, but by comparing and sharing these problems we may be able to understand better our own situations.

Mother at Home

Families with the mother staying home full time are no longer in the majority. According to one estimate, in only seven percent of American families is Father the breadwinner and Mother at home with the kids. It may seem at first that among those in this seven percent at least the grandparents' role would not have changed much, but this is not true.

Isolated in the suburbs

Consider the example of parents Judy and Joe and the grandparents closest to them, May and Will. (We met May and Will in Chapter One.) Their family relationships are traditional in form but not in substance. Judy, a full-time housewife, lives in Calgary with Joe and two small children. She had a job but gave it up to raise the children. Joe is getting ahead in a middle-management position in a big company. They live in a little house in the suburbs. Will and May live in Thunder Bay, a few hundred miles away.

Joe leaves the house early in the morning and often brings home a briefcase full of work at night. Most of the neighboring couples have jobs. Judy has chosen full-time parenting as her career, at least for a few years, but she is lonely and bored. An educated, intelligent young woman, she misses the job she had before the arrival of the children. Now she has little social involvement; there's not even a shopping center conveniently nearby. She and Joe considered buying a second car for Judy's use but decided it was not a priority in their limited budget.

Their tiny household is typical. Their house was available and within their means, but there is little room for Judy to develop the hobbies for which she might otherwise find some time, and the house lacks a decent basement where Joe can work. There is no room to accommodate visiting grandparents, who are fond of their grandchildren and would like to see more of them.

It used to be taken for granted that a mother in Judy's position would carry on her child-care and housekeeping tasks, finding time during the day for socializing with neighbors and friends. But it is not easy to make friends on a street where most of the neighbors are away all day. Friends they have made through Joe's job live in high-rise apartments in other parts of the city. Judy would be glad to be involved in part-time work, volunteer or paid, or go back to school, but she lacks initiative. Or maybe it is the money she lacks. Good baby-sitters are expensive and hard to find. A new community center will open in a year or so with classes Judy would enjoy, and with baby-sitting. She looks forward to this, but in the meantime, she keeps her troubles to herself. May and Will have noticed Judy's lack of enthusiasm in her letters and have a feeling of foreboding about the marriage.

May and Will are uncertain how to help. They could offer financial assistance but have hesitated to intrude, remembering their own reluctance to call on their parents for help. May considers taking a bus to Calgary to spend a few days with her daughter, reducing her loneliness. May would not mind sleeping on a couch. She and Will might even stay for a weekend in a motel near Judy and Joe's home, a motel with a swimming pool where they could entertain their grandchildren. They could offer to stay with the children while Judy went to town to shop. This situation doesn't quite fit the picture of an old-style family reunion, but the effort to connect would be the same.

Back home May and Will might try developing a more active correspondence with the grandchildren, keeping in touch with their developing interests. We could all think of other suggestions that would help. The way to keep in touch is to do it, not just wish we could.

New baby and poor

Marilyn and Steve are new parents with a three-month-old baby. They face many uncertainties. Marilyn, who stays at home, has worries about her husband's insecure employment. She is aware that her education was limited, cut short by pregnancy. She is reluctant to relieve her stress by sharing problems with family members or intimate friends. She gets depressed easily. Television plays too large a part in her life—she uses it as a substitute for human companionship. Boredom sets in, and initiative dwindles.

Grandparents find such situations worrisome. Relieving boredom is a good goal. Some of us are able to help by dropping in on our children occasionally to talk about the baby. Marilyn needs help and advice, but she is so emotionally vulnerable that it is difficult to communicate with her. Anything that borders on criticism hurts. Small negative suggestions, like "Don't you think the baby should be getting more fresh air?" are taken as questioning her know-how about child rearing. At some point her mother might be able to help her gain her perspective about herself by suggesting that: "Babyhood doesn't last forever," but this kind of advice should be reserved for an appropriate, comfortable time.

The grandparents could also suggest outside contacts and interests, provided they can help Marilyn devise ways to free herself for the time she would need to be away from home. If she would like to take a course to get ahead with her education perhaps Grandma or Grandpa could look after the baby one or two half-days a week, or even pay for the class. In the past, getting out of the poverty circle was often impossible. Today, however, courses and job retraining are more available.

Though casual visiting and some basic sitting might help Marilyn, some grandparents do not have the time to help. One grandmother I know, Nella, is divorced and working at a physically exhausting job. She finds it difficult to respond to her young family's request for baby-sitting, or even just to drop in. She is too tired, although she adores her new granddaughter. She wonders whether to suggest a better time slot when she would not be so tired, or an alternative arrangement—perhaps her son could bring the baby to her instead of her having to go by bus to their place. Nella should take this initiative. She could explain her preference with a simple phone call. Enjoying her granddaughter alone for a while is good therapy for Nella and, although she and her young family are both at the poverty level, there are some positive, helpful things to do. Do it, Nella!

Two Working Parents

Families with two working parents are a much more familiar pattern today. Their numbers have risen in response to the rising cost of living and the demand for women in the work force. Among mothers of children younger than three in Canada, it is estimated that one out of four has a job outside the home.

Busy, busy parents

Gordon and his wife, Tamara—we met them in Chapter Two—have two children, ages five and seven, and both parents work. Gordon is the son of Robin, a Widowed and Helpful grandmother. In Chapter Two we saw some of her difficulties in dealing with widowhood and loneliness.

Robin's relationship to the family is shaped by the fast pace at which Gordon and Tamara and the children must move through each day of the week. Robin's solutions are sensible and sensitive, organized around her own part-time job. Living alone in the old family house, Robin has figured out ways of seeing the children fairly frequently. She is careful to fit in with their changing schedules, and she invites them one at a time when possible. She visits her grandchildren at *their* home only when Gordon or Tamara suggest it or when a sitter arrangement breaks down.

Out-of-town job

When one of the two working parents has an out-of-town job, life becomes even more complicated. We met Paul and Wendy in Chapter Two—Wendy's mother, Sylva, is an Eager Beaver. Paul leaves home Sunday night and returns Friday evening to his family. His wife, Wendy, is struggling with a burdensome office job. She comes home each night to the demands of raising their two children. By the weekend she is ready for some spousal support. Paul tries not to be too tired to deal with the children and has given up golf for the time being, but sometimes he feels a little inept. Wendy and the nanny are in charge during the week, and the children question Paul's authority during the weekends.

These parents face strenuous demands. Each of them is committed, but they bicker about little things more than they used to. They are deeply in love, but romance flowers best when it is not hurried: they wish they had more time.

Leo and Sylva, the grandparents, are concerned and responsible people with good judgment. They want to do what they can to help while making a minimum of demands on this little family, which they treasure. On weekends they visit Paul and Wendy only briefly, if at all. If one of the children gets sick Grandma Sylva volunteers to help. Grandpa Leo runs a few errands. During the week, Sylva and Leo may take Wendy and the children out for a meal. More often, they offer to sit with the children on a weekday evening to allow Wendy to go out. Wendy's escape valve is folkdancing at the local recreation center. Leo and Sylva have occasionally had friends in to play a few rubbers of bridge at Wendy's house while Wendy has gone to her dance class.

Three young families for Grandmother

My friend Fiona, who is the grandmother of three sets of grandchildren in three families with two working parents, finds it difficult to maintain satisfactory contact. She finally gave up trying to make appointments with the grandchildren and came up with a new idea. She announced that, on the fourth Sunday of every month, she would have a dinner at her place. Any members of the family who were free were welcome. She asked them to let her know twenty-four hours in advance. The attendance varies, but the arrangement has worked out well. If she finds there is going to be a crowd, she turns the meal into a buffet or backyard picnic; ten or fewer and she has a sit-down dinner.

At present Fiona's son, daughter-in-law and twin three-year-old grandsons are living with her for two months while their house is being renovated. Though she is assisting them in a major way, she says: "I don't do much. I let them help. They take turns preparing meals. The twins never stop exploring, and I let them. They're into clothes, pictures, hiding places, sandbox play, sink play. I am thrilled that they are here. I often baby-sit at night, but I don't try to organize them. I see one twin taking the lead one day and the other one the next day. It's perfectly fascinating. I'm pretty busy with my own affairs but when I'm at home I'm available. Their parents are responsible, so I feel relaxed and fortunate. I am really getting to know the twins."

In households with two working parents, communication is top priority. Grandparents must know what is needed and when it is needed. Wading in without a clear sense of the family schedules and routines can play havoc. Taking some initiative to discuss plans with the parents and the grandchildren pays off.

Common-Law Parents

Grandparents may find it more difficult to sort out their feelings about a family when the parents have not married. Georgie and her partner, Michael, have a two-year-old son.

Georgie and Michael both work; they intend their arrangement to be a continuing one. For their own reasons they have decided not to get married, a choice that does not concern their close friends or their employers. They are responsible adults whose views about marriage are carefully thought out. Both of them were in university at a time when questions were being raised about established institutions and authority. Since then they have seen the bitterness and turmoil of numerous divorces and have decided to stay clear of a formal marriage arrangement.

Common-law marriages are fairly prevalent today, one estimate suggesting that one-third of marriages are common-law. Many common-law marriages are more casual than Georgie's and Michael's, and many follow separations and divorce.

This family has some problems. One is Grandpa Bob. Bob, Georgie's father, was happily married; he and his wife believed in the sanctity of marriage. In their time, there were several fates worse than death from which daughters were to be saved, and one of them was to bear a child out of wedlock. Bob finds it difficult to face the fact that Georgie has chosen not to marry. Georgie remembers her early teaching, and it leads her into some inhibitions in her relationship with Bob. Both of them need help because, underneath the frictions, they love each other.

Grandfather Bob was chatting with a friend one day: "I dream of having more fun with grandchildren. So far I have one and I don't see him often enough." Georgie is looking for a better-paying job. She is living in a small apartment with her partner, and their child is in day care. Georgie says she can manage, but Bob is not sure what this means. He wonders if it means that she does not want his help. The truth is that Georgie is as harried as any working mother and would like to have some financial help but she feels reluctant to involve her father because she senses Bob's disapproval of her life-style.

Bob has not gotten beyond his deep suspicion of Michael, whom he still regards as Georgie's boyfriend. Bob has not tried very hard to establish any relationship with Michael. He made a serious mistake on one occasion—he invited Georgie and the baby to his cottage, and he did not ask Michael. Georgie went because she thought it might be good for the child. She also needed a holiday, and she wanted an opportunity to see something of her father. Once there, however, they argued about Georgie's living arrangements then fell into an uncomfortable silence; she left earlier than she had planned. The effect was to set up a wall between Bob and his young family.

Bob needs to decide which is the more important to him, his old concepts or his relationship with his daughter and grandson. If he could bring himself to think clearly about this I feel sure which he would choose: he would accept Michael and make an effort to get to know him. This gesture would open the door to seeing his grandson and to helping his daughter. Georgie would benefit also from some clear thinking. Georgie's arrangement with Michael is causing problems between her and her father, and this friction is, in turn, causing problems between Georgie and Michael. Unfounded assumptions on both sides preclude comfortable communication.

Older Parents

We find a rather different family pattern in older parents who decide to have children later in life, after their careers are established or because they have entered into a new marriage and want to have a child together. Such families are becoming more common these days. When older parents are pushing baby carriages, we look twice to observe whether they are parents or grandparents. Indeed, some are both, because they have children from an earlier marriage.

Grandparenting in the older parent family will take on a slightly different character when their new baby arrives. If they are already grandparents, the new arrival will probably not evoke the sense of being needed that the earlier grandchildren did. The couple may have built-in baby-sitters or helpers in the older children from previous marriages. Older parents are probably not isolated and insecure, emotionally or financially, and will not be as dependent on the grandparents. The grandparents therefore will have an easier time of it and may probably enjoy grandparenting even more.

The maturity of the parents makes possible a more open, equal relationship with grandparents. But it is not always easy. Older children may feel resentment and intrusion into their lives, and grandparents may then be hesitant to take initiatives. In addition the grandparents in these cases are usually older. They may have more physical limitations than younger grandparents.

The Single-Parent Family

Some single-parent families start out as two-parent families. Separation or the death of a spouse can leave one parent to carry on. Other single-parent families start out that way either because an unmarried woman has an unplanned pregnancy and decides to keep her baby or because a single woman decides to get pregnant. In all these cases there is a lot grandparents can do to help and support the young family.

Lots of grandparents are reluctant to accept the single-parent scenario. Major differences can arise between generations when children are born out of wedlock. Grandparents would do well to face the situation, if necessary with professional counseling, because letting feelings harden can only create heartbreaking isolation, especially if the single parent is a young mother who is engulfed in emotional, financial and physical difficulties.

Unmarried teenage parent

In these instances, grandparents quite often find themselves called upon to act as proxy parents. Al and Vi received a clarion call from their sixteen-year-old daughter, Gill, who had been living with a boyfriend for the summer. They responded by taking Gill back home with them.

For three months after the birth of Bobby, Grandpa Al and Grandma Vi looked after him most of the time, giving Gill time to find a job and an apartment. Then Gill left the grandparents' home, taking Bobby with her. Shortly after they moved out, Vi discovered that her daughter could not cope with her new setup and that the baby was being neglected. Gill's apartment was noisy and dirty, not fit for an infant. Her pals were coming and going at all hours. After two months Gill needed to be rescued again.

Reluctantly she accepted her parents' offer. With Gill's written consent, Al and Vi went through the necessary legal procedures and took Bobby as their own. Quite a proposition, for grandparents to become parents again!

When Bobby was two years old, Gill reclaimed her son. Gill and Bobby are now living with Gill's older sister. It was not easy for Al and Vi; they feared there would be more neglect. After careful discussion with Gill and with a social worker, they finally accepted the situation. Al and Vi, already overburdened with eight children and ten grandchildren, have strained their budget to include support for Bobby in a private nursery school. He has a special place in their hearts, and in his extended family.

For single parents in crisis, total grandparent involvement may be the only appropriate response. Not all situations call for such extreme measures, however. Some young women rise to the occasion and provide excellent care for their children. For such women the emotional support grandparents provide is often the most important contribution.

Too long in the nest

After her divorce, Rita and her three children moved in with her mother and father, Mila and Rick. The grandparents gave their all to support their vulnerable young family, even financing the children's education. Rita had a job but little opportunity for an independent life, especially since she was shy about bringing men friends home. Instead, she clung to her parents and children. Mila became involved in her daughter's world, giving her detailed directions as to how to run her life, along with manifestations of maternal love more appropriate for a teenager. Fifteen years later, Mila, now widowed, is dependent on Rita and the grandchildren.

Neither woman has developed other interests or job skills. Both of them are stuck in a groove.

Clearly, both women and the grandchildren would be further ahead today if Rita had been less dependent on her parents. Some parents tend to offer their adult child more care than is healthy for the independence of the young family. While Rick and Mila deserve full credit for giving help and shelter to Rita, it would have been better if they had also encouraged her to establish an independent life as soon as possible.

Weaned in time

Grandparents Helen and Jim faced a similar situation but followed a more constructive path, helping their child to a life of her own. Helen and Jim had retired to a southern town where they could enjoy golf and live within a short distance of their daughter, Nora, and her family. When Nora and her husband separated five years later, she and her kids moved in with Helen and Jim.

They all got along together and willingly made the necessary compromises in their living arrangements. After a year or so, Nora pulled herself together and decided to start a new life. Helen and Jim encouraged her and extended some financial help. Taking her six-year-old daughter and four-year-old son with her, Nora moved to her childhood hometown where she found a part-time job at the library. She soon regained her self-confidence.

Helen would have liked to have held on to Nora and the grandchildren, but Nora's release made her life more meaningful. Helen and Jim got back to spending more time on the golf course. "Jim really did resent the time I spent with the children, which would otherwise have been my time with him," says Helen. The two families continue to visit, and sometimes the grandchildren visit Helen and Jim one at a time.

Grandparents in the dark

This is a simple story in which it appears by hindsight that it would have been better for the separating couple to divulge the facts to the grandparents sooner and more fully. Fran was thunderstruck when her daughter, Susan, told her that she and her husband were separating. Fran thought they had settled in for a long, loving marriage such as hers had been with Dan. It seemed her heartache would never stop. Fran asked Susan why the explosive announcement had been kept from her until it had become final. Her daughter explained that she wanted to avoid hurting her mother and had feared her parents might try to persuade her to stay in the marriage. Susan wanted to shield herself from her mother's tears during a period when her own emotions were running high.

The grandparents' distress was exacerbated by shock; they had failed to see any signs of the impending separation. A major task for them was to deal with their own feelings without imposing them on the parents and children. Eventually, they did accept the separation as final. The most they could do, they realized, was to offer to take the grandchildren for whatever time was helpful, and to help their daughter assemble her new living arrangements.

The mother quit

This story is quite different; here a mother deserted her children, leaving her spouse to cope. This is not the more usual case where a mother leaves the family for a short time, meaning to return and having no serious doubt about the eventual custody of her children. In this traumatic story Catherine decided to leave her children as well as her husband, Jed. Here the grandmother is Edna, Catherine's mother, and her role turned out to be crucial.

Edna was very fond of Jed, and after Catherine left she set herself the task of helping Jed as much as she could. She assisted with the cooking, shopping and after-school playtime, always involving the three children in these tasks. She and Jed did not live in the same house, but Edna had a special one-to-one relationship with each person in that family. It grew in depth, and each person depended on the love and support of the others. Jed asked for Edna's advice on such things as discipline, and they worked creatively together. Catherine eventually remarried, and after five years of separation from her children she started seeing them again, but the families remained independent.

Following the initial shock of her daughter's desertion and her own struggle to restore torn feelings of love for her daughter and the family she left, Edna began to experience deep satisfaction in this unusual family life. She has her own friends, but her grandchildren are her great joy. This is not a normal family (what is normal today?), but it has sustained and enriched the lives of all concerned. Perhaps the key to Edna's response is threefold: she didn't blame Jed for the breakdown of the marriage; she appreciates the fact that Jed fully accepts her; and she found herself able to forgive her daughter.

Day Care

Day-care centers are filled largely with children of working-parent and single-parent families. When parents work away from home they entrust their children to day care, pre-schools, nannies or sitters. These alternative forms of child care provide supportive services for working parents and relieve grandparents of many baby-sitting responsibilities.

Day-care facilities are burgeoning, some of them good and others not so good. Interested grandparents should inform themselves about the standards and the program of the day-care center their grandchild attends. Their knowledge and involvement are particularly useful when the parents are too busy to visit the center regularly. Some day-care centers, public-school kindergarten and primary classes welcome grandparents who are willing to spend time with the children. Grandparents give the children a feeling of support that is often missing from their homes. Grandparents can also help transport their own grandchildren to and from the day-care center, a chore many parents find arduous.

In this new family pattern grandparents do not act as parents; rather, their role is supportive. They should remain in the background. If they have questions about the quality of the day-care center, they should relay them to the parents and leave it to them to clear any issues with the director.

A good day-care program can enrich your grandchild's life and add interest to your life, as well. A few days ago I observed the preparations for a well-conceived party at the YMCA. Parents and grandparents were invited to come along with the children. While the party was in progress, I noticed some of the children had nobody attached to them. I suppose their mothers were working, and perhaps they didn't have grandmothers. By then I was in a hurry but would have enjoyed staying to act as a proxy grandmother for one of those kids. Perhaps there is the germ of a good idea in this.

Mixed Marriages

Increasingly, people of our children's generation and our grandchildren's are choosing to marry outside their culture, race or religion. Mixed marriages are not easy for parents or grandparents. Blacks, whites, Christians, Jews, Moslems: all find difficulty in melding.

People of many races and cultures crisscross each other's lives every day. More of the young are learning languages other than their own. Business is organizing itself internationally. Events of significance to Canada take place in Tokyo or Bujumbura, and we hear about them right away. Immigrants of every color and religion have settled in our cities. It is hardly surprising that mixed marriages are more common.

If one of your children decides upon a mixed marriage there is no reason to be surprised or ashamed if your first reactions are negative. If she goes ahead, you know that she will have to make compromises and adapt to her husband's culture, as he will to hers. The marriage may appear to be a leap into the unknown, and you all want to shield your young from dangers. If you find that the culture into which your child marries seems to exclude yours, or if you find its political or religious beliefs disturbing, you have added reasons to be distressed.

But it is pointless to worry in advance. Your son-in-law is a person, not just an alien stereotype. If it were otherwise, why would your daughter choose him? When we take positive action to affirm common human bonds, the results are usually rewarding. Prejudice breaks down with familiarity, and we learn to respect people whose roots are different from ours. The habits of faraway peoples becomes meshed into ours. A mixed marriage is likely to demand purpose and stamina in addition to love, but it can enrich both families.

For grandparents to adjust to simple matters of different housekeeping arrangements and food preferences is both a challenge and an opportunity. Grandma Michelle had very tentative reactions to the mixed marriage in her own family. Her son-in-law comes from Mexico. She comes from a rural community in eastern Canada and moved in with her daughter's family in midtown Toronto after she was widowed. She said, "I can't pronounce the names of the hot sauces that my grandchildren keep putting on strange dishes. Thank goodness we all like bananas."

Michelle told me: "Emotional outpourings were certainly difficult for me to absorb in my new family and neighborhood. Some European and Caribbean families do much more hugging, celebrating, weeping and yelling than I was accustomed to. There are differences in respect to discipline, and my Mexican son-in-law shares the attitudes of our neighbors; they are completely relaxed in guiding their children. I am learning that my old stricter methods of discipline are not as effective as I used to think. I know I was full of prejudice when I first arrived in this new community with all its cultural difference. I am beginning to realize that I can make a go of it."

Then there is Grandma Marg, a citizen of the world, whose late husband had a distinguished career that took them to many countries. Her son, an educator, lives and works in Africa with his lovely black African wife. Marg's two granddaughters have spent time with her in Canada. During that time they were fortunate to be part of a receptive extended family. They spent weekends with Marg while attending a boarding school just out of the city; they visited their uncles and aunts in other parts of the country during vacations. They have now rejoined their parents in Africa. Marg's adjustments to her grandchildren's living patterns are creative and comfortable.

She says: "Some of us are lucky enough to have a connection, through our grandchildren, to another culture. The differences and similarities of child rearing stretch our thinking and our flexibility. Does it really matter what time our children go to bed, except for the convenience of the adults? Nutrition is available in many food combinations, and what joy to be able to indulge the child's curiosity and appreciation of the new and different by serving attractively presented surprises at the grandparents' house from time to time."

Grandparents who are recent immigrants struggle with culture shock and language. "Mostly they are lonely," wrote Dorothy Lipovenko in the Toronto *Globe and Mail* (January 6, 1989). She quoted a teacher who works with Chinese women: "It's very hard for them to find someone to listen to their problems....Emotionally, they are starving. It is a hole their children cannot fill because they are unwilling or have no time." Of older men she said, "They expect to be consulted but their advice may be out of step. There may be a real power loss. In the old country, the elderly are the most important people in their family. Here, they find themselves really dependent on their children."

Grandparents who emigrate are people who have experienced a great deal of change. A variety of different forces has played upon their lives. They are usually strong and enduring people. On the whole the relationship between generations is intimate and close. But cultural habits of the older generation are sometimes at odds with the experience and expectations of the young. Grandchildren feel excited about a modern life-style, and are frequently restless at home, causing friction between the generations.

Loneliness and loss of power can usually be alleviated if the grandparents can talk with each other and share their problems and interests. Some grandparents, after they have been helped by language classes, are prepared to walk their grandchildren to school; some become safety guards, patrolling children at street crossings; some begin to participate in cultural activities. Others share in community recreation programs.

Mixed marriages and mixed cultures can flourish. Modern grandparents can help in the process, and immigrant grandparents can make a great contribution in passing on the old culture.

Gay Parents

One of the family patterns grandparents may deal with today is that of the gay couple as parents. As this sexual orientation becomes more acceptable in our society, our children may decide not only to live with a same-sex partner, but to have or to keep children in the relationship. Quite often, women will not discover until after they have already married and had children that their needs for partnership lie elsewhere. In the past, women who decided to leave their marriages for this reason almost inevitably lost their children in custody battles, but in recent times the courts have begun to see things differently. Gay fathers, too, may need to leave their marriages for similar reasons, but they may want to retain full or partial custody of their children.

Grandparents in this situation must struggle to contain any shock or dismay they may feel: maintaining communication and contact is far less painful than the loss of a relationship with a child and grandchildren. A grandparent's first reaction may be guilt or shame, but this, too, must be managed. No one knows exactly how anyone comes to have a particular sexual orientation, only that it is not within the person's own control, gay or straight.

As with any kind of family breakup, grandparents can help most by maintaining a steady, nonjudgmental relationship with the grandchildren, making it clear that their love for the grandchildren and for the children's parents remains unabated.

Lesbians in stable partnerships (or even those who remain single) may decide to become parents, through adoption or insemination. Grandparents then have various new relationships to consider, not only with their daughter and her child, but with the daughter's partner and the child's biological father. Lesbians who choose to have children with a partner generally see the partner as a full parent, just as a spouse would be. Grandparents should take their cues from their daughter, asking directly how best to include her partner and the child's biological father into the family. In this case our best guess may not be good enough.

Similarly, if a lesbian daughter tells her parents that she plans to become a co-parent, her parents need to ascertain whether she hopes they will see themselves as the child's grandparents. If in doubt, assume that she does. They may soon find themselves as biological grandparents as well; in some lesbian couples, both partners have children.

Grandparents may have a variety of concerns about a lesbian daughter's choices—they may worry about the grandchild's adjustment, about whether the child will be teased in school for having two mothers—but women normally do not take such a step without careful thought about these very issues. If you want to know how your daughter plans to handle matters such as these, ask—but with interest, not with horror.

Usually the biological mother and her partner must work full-time: women's wages are often lower than men's, and so a woman is less likely to be able to support another woman while she stays home with a child. Depending to some extent on where they live, these parents do not get normal family benefits or medical insurance. Grandparents can help in whatever way they are able—this family will need the same kind of assistance as any family with two working parents.

Gay men are also likely to be parents. If you are the grandparent in such a situation, your involvement, I suggest, is the same as in any other grandparental relationship with a grandchild. What is hard on grandparents is when a father leaves a family to enter into a new relationship with a gay partner. It is possible that he might take his children with him, although it is more usual to leave the children with the mother; sometimes all ties with the father are severed. The father, of course, might have joint custody or access. Grandparents in such situations can play a vitally supportive role both directly with their grandchildren and indirectly in supporting their adult children.

Parents Unemployed and Parents in School

These social categories are on the increase today, and their numbers are such as to make another category of parental living arrangements. These arrangements probably fluctuate more than the ones we have already discussed.

Grandparents' relationships with the families of students or of unemployed young parents will depend on the degree to which the grandparents become involved in child care and on the parents' use of day care. Some of these family groups choose to live in a cooperative housing arrangement with other young families, making grandparent connections a little awkward. In the case of students, their timetables for classes define the family routine but often conflict with grandparents' schedules.

The emotional stress in a family where unemployment hovers affects grandparents. The subtleties of our relationships with our adult children are such that we can handle the issue only with great care and good communication. Some financial assistance may allow your children a little more independence.

No matter what the parents' living arrangements, some things remain the same. To be effective grandparents and to make the most of their relationship with the grandchildren, grandparents need open minds and a willingness to communicate and compromise. Finding a role to play in today's busy young families sometimes takes imagination and perserverance, but we all should have learned a few of those tricks by now.

7

Separation and Divorce

There is a saying that divorce is harder on the grandparents than on the parents. I think it wrong. To ask who is most affected is like asking who has the sorest back or who is bravest. Grandparents are deeply involved, but so are others. The fact is that separation and divorce are attended by periods of dark and bitter readjustment for the husband and wife, for the children and for the grandparents.

Grandparents do not cause the rupture of families—or, I should add, not often—but they do get caught up in the consequences, living arrangements, money problems, personal adjustments and rearrangements of friendships.

When a family separates, everyone concerned is hurt and confused at first; grandparents are no exception. But both parents and grandparents should do all they can to avoid damage to the children. Our hearts go out to the children, and this is good, because many things are happening at once and there is a lot to think about and to do. Unless the children are a high priority in everyone's mind, they can get lost in the shuffle.

There is no need to be pessimistic. Children are hardy and adaptable creatures and they survive. We all see many children whose parents are divorced. Can you tell the difference between these kids and others? Not by appearance or the way they play in the school yard or dash around the streets, and not by success in school. The children of broken families have to make difficult adjustments but they can do it. For now, we can be confident that our grandchildren will probably be okay.

There is, however, a strong link between single mothers and poverty, and a link between poverty and failures of various kinds. Grandparents may be more urgently challenged to help in meeting this trauma in the family life of their children.

Understanding Divorce

Separation and divorce are becoming more frequent. Why is this, and what has changed? The biggest change is that women are more free to choose. Ideas have changed, as well. There is nothing new about bad marriages; history and novels are replete with them. Not may years ago, however, couples tried harder to stay together, either because their society left them no choice or because they believed it was best for the children. Now they are more likely to realize they are not doing the children a favor by sticking to a loveless, unhappy or confrontational marriage.

Separations take place for various reasons. The husband and wife may have gradually drifted apart into two solitudes. One of the partners may have found a fulfilling relationship or an irresistible attraction to someone else. Or there may be other reasons: emotional or physical abuse, alcoholism, emotional immaturity, financial irresponsibility or incombatibility.

Separations take different forms. The partners may lose interest in each other gradually, without quite realizing what is happening until one of them makes the break. The whole thing may be conducted in a calm atmosphere of discussion and negotiation of arrangements. It is more usual for the spouses to allow disappointments and frustrations to accumulate until one of them suddenly erupts. I must add that I have never known of a separation without acrimony.

The tensions during the buildup to separation involve all members of the family. Children respond with anger, grief or relief. Most important to them are the changes in the hitherto secure (although perhaps increasingly combative) family environment that has nurtured them.

Animosity between the former spouses tends to persist after a divorce, and this infects other family relationships. Grandparents may be in for a short or prolonged period of separation from a son-in-law or daughter-in-law. If new partnerships develop we may become step-grandparents, with even more grandchildren than before. All this is easier when there is joint custody, but simple it is not.

Grandparents' Part

There are better and worse ways for grandparents to try to preserve their relationships with their families. If, for example, a grandmother has strong views against divorce, as many do, she would be well advised to consider how strongly and when to assert her beliefs. The danger is that she may only cause more turmoil for a daughter who has thought long and hard about leaving her husband and has finally done it.

Grandparents get caught in the aftershocks. Confronted with the breakdown of a marriage, they are affected immediately. One grandfather who had lived in Central America likened the sensation to being in an earthquake. Surroundings suddenly become unfamiliar, and nothing is dependably stable. Grandparents suffer for a number of reasons. It may be that the grandparent has never lost the parental instinct and wants to protect his own young, even after they have grown up. It may be that divorce spells trouble, and he shrinks from what his offspring are getting into. It may be that he seeks stability as he gets older, and divorce implies the reverse. He may know that divorce is expensive for all concerned, including him. It may be that he felt close to this young couple as a unit and was shaken to learn that the tensions between them were worse than he had thought.

To an arm's length observer, one more separation or divorce is just another statistic added to an already large number. To those immediately affected, the splitting of a family is a major crisis for the spouses, children and grandparents.

In the presence of a fracturing family, many grandparents wish they could take positive affirmative action. The truth is that there is nothing much that a grandparent can do. Grandparents cannot reglue the marriage, and it would be dumb to try.

During the early shock phase the grandparent, however, can play a useful role. It's such a passive and simple one that it may not seem like much. The parents need understanding and hugs. Grandchildren need assurance that they are going to be taken care of and that they are loved. No one needs grandparents to impose emotional displays along with twenty-twenty hindsight. If grandparents can remain calm and helpful, they can be confident that their self-discipline will be remembered and appreciated.

Some grandparents customarily react to bad news with strong emotional displays, however, and they have only themselves to blame if their children fail to confide fully in them. A daughter in the midst of divorce proceedings is sufficiently charged with her own painful emotions that she naturally becomes defensive and self-protective.

One grandfather I know reacted with anger when his daughter told him she was leaving her husband. He loves his daughter but he was also on very good terms with his son-in-law. He had developed a false sense of security about their home and about his grandchildren. He felt at the time as if something was being done to him, and he resented it. Of course, something was being done to him. That wasn't the purpose of his daughter's plan. Now, some years later, he looks back on the experience with regret. At a time when his daughter desperately needed sympathy and assurance, he was thinking only about himself. He can see clearly that he was unavailable to her in a time of need. Now he wishes he had done it differently.

Few people react best when they are surprised, and separation often takes grandparents by surprise. A married couple moving toward separation should bring grandparents into the picture as promptly, frankly and factually as possible. Not many do, however. One trouble is that the couple is not always able to alert the grandparents in advance because one of the spouses may take the other by surprise. Or they may wish to protect the grandparents or themselves.

Life is so intense at the time of separation that grandparents can hardly be foremost in the minds of the parents. Grandparents find that the two who are separating tend to shield their parents from the full impact of the situation. This makes things worse and increases the grandparents' anxieties.

It is best to remember that the spouses are under the most extreme emotional pressures. One of them has chosen a new course of action. They know they are moving into something new and unknown, and they are full of trepidation. They feel driven by events.

People under extreme pressure do not behave entirely rationally. In the heat of the moment anyone is prone to make mistakes. Separating parents may not yet have reached agreement about custody of the children, and there may be anxiety on that score. Both parents are leaving much behind, perhaps ownership of the home, other assets and joint living arrangements. They may give no thought to the costs of separation or divorce, or they underestimate them. They live from one day to the next and they do the things they have to do.

After Divorce

A divorce changes lots of things for lots of people—and many of those changes affect the grandparents. When there are two sets of grandparents, more often than not they have had a cordial relationship with one another. When the couple splits, relations between the grandparents can become difficult. The grandparents get different accounts of what has happened. Tension and differences in perception are understandable. They may eventually get back on an easy footing, but in the first stages of a breakup, little can be resolved. During these painful periods for grandparents, spouses and children, the main thing is to avoid using the children as conduits for your views.

Married couples form friendships with other couples, and grandparents often participate in these. When a couple separates, the friends tend to take sides, his or hers. The husband continues to see some friends; the wife sees others. This taking of sides has an effect on grandparents, too. Older people do not tend to pick up new acquaintances as easily as they did earlier.

Grandparents will be drawn into different roles in the aftermath of a separation if their son or daughter is left as a single parent. When the parent is a young mother, for example, she may be engulfed in emotional and financial difficulties. Most grandparents are reluctant to accept the single-parent scenario but they can usually learn to be constructive about it. The problems are endless: shelter, organization of time and money. Single mothers have to get the children to child care before work and arrange after-school transportation. Grandparents can offer to assist with the endless tasks if they are able. If the grandparents are clumsy about it, they may become part of the problem rather than part of the solution.

What about the Children?

Grandparents make themselves most useful by providing images of continuity in a world that is falling apart. Sometimes it is desirable for grandparents to take care of the children during the upheaval. When children have been well-loved and nurtured, they can usually make a good adjustment. The experience of family separation is traumatic, and the adjustment may take some time. A grandparent may have strong feelings about the in-law who left. If so, it is well to keep in mind that it is scary stuff for a grandchild to be told that Granny hates his father.

Children are emotionally bruised by the breakup. You might think guilt feelings are widespread enough without children putting themselves into convicts' row, but many think the troubles between Dad and Mom are their fault. This widespread phenomenon can be explained at many psychological levels. A Freudian might say that little girls want their parents' marriage to end so they can have their daddy, and little boys want the marriage to end so they can have their mother. Then when it *does* end, it's easy to fear they did it.

A grandparent may find a grandchild uncommunicative. A grandson may avoid eye contact because he doesn't want to be seen crying or otherwise to reveal himself. He resents the change that has been thrust upon him and he finds difficulty in expressing it. He may conceal it but eventually he will spill it all out, to a parent, grandparent or close friend. If he chooses you, the grandparent, for this purpose, you are entitled to be gratified and not to worry if some of the anger is directed at you. This is entirely normal, and there is no need to worry about it. The best thing is to be available and to be patient.

Sometimes it is possible to devise situations in which the children will open up. One woman spoke of her experience with her granddaughter in a way that might give the rest of us a hint. "As we drove in the car, if she sat in the backseat, we could discuss many things as long as it was not face to face!" Another grandmother took a different tack. She found that she and her granddaughter could use puppets as intermediaries and have all kinds of important conversations.

New Connections and Remarriage

After divorce there is the period of being single. Single parenting with full or joint custody of the children is an outcome we discussed in Chapter Five. As time passes, the former spouses meet new friends and enter into new relationships. They may be just that—new relationships with no permanent attachments. Or more permanent living arrangements may develop that constitute, in all but name, a marriage. And then there may be legal remarriage. The remarriage or a new permanent connection for a son or daughter opens up new doors for the grandparent.

New marriage relationships can provide a wonderful opportunity for a fresh start and mutual fulfillment after an unhappy marriage has been left behind. Responsible new partners take on board for this voyage not only their new intimate personal relationship but also a whole set of relationships connected with their new spouse's friends and relatives.

Steps

For stepparents, however, one major task is so big that it dwarfs the others, namely, to gain the confidence of the children. The grandparent can help enormously in this. She can operate in two directions. And she can let her grandchildren see that she accepts the new stepfather in every way.

She can make herself available to her new family as friend and confidante.

A child in a remarriage may well be carrying a big load of resentment, and he may be inclined to take some of it out on the new stepparent. He did not choose the rearrangement of family life; it just happened to him. In the formation of new intimate partnerships, including remarriage, children and grandparents are the recipients of a fait accompli. They have had no decision in this very important happening in their lives and yet they are faced with many new relationships.

Older children who were aware for some time of the estrangement between their natural parents may recognize that the separation was a good thing. Possibly not even then, though, is the reality of the remarriage fully accepted.

With luck and good management, however, children will like their new stepparent, new grandparents, stepsisters and stepbrothers. And with luck and good management, the grandparents will like their new daughter-in-law or son-in-law, their new grandchildren and the new co-grandparents. That's a lot of new relationships to absorb. It calls for *lots* of good luck and good management. It would not be surprising if the remarrieds chose to give priority to their immediate family and took a little less time for grandparents.

Grandparents who are sensitively attuned to the new setup are able to wait a while and let the initiative for participation come from the new family. We will learn to treat our new grandchildren naturally and with great interest. Nobody expects perfect responses, but making an effort to relate comfortably and supportively is the only way to get to first base. As with any relationship, time, communication and planning are important.

Remarried Grandparents

Remarriage of grandparents can result in separating a grandchild from a beloved grandparent. A new spouse for Grandpa following a divorce or a death can lead to resettling, perhaps in a faraway place, which takes little account of the family left behind. If the older remarrieds, caught up in their new romance, forget their other vital family connections, it can seem unfair to a grandchild.

I know one newly married couple who moved to a retirement community in the south. The family they left behind is suffering from this abrupt change. "It feels like personal surgery to no longer have the intimate relationship we and our children once enjoyed," the parent said to me. "They seem to have forgotten us and never take the initiative in suggesting a visit for one of the kids."

Family relationships need to be handled delicately after separations and new connections. Alienating our tenderest connections—our grandchildren—can be hurtful. We grandparents could consider quiet or even active expressions of continuing love, ones that hold the door open to more participation in family affairs in the future.

With all these changes, it is best to stress the positive. Most grandparents, in spite of their limitations, try to relate to their grandchildren and stepgrandchildren in positive ways. Good parent-grandchild-grandparent communication can smooth troubled waters and lead to some wonderful times together.

8

Grandchildren Visit Grandparents

Clamorous offstage noises, high-pitched and getting louder as they approach. They sound friendly. We open the front door to find it is not a mob but, instead, two excited grandchildren arriving to stay for a couple of days. They are duly escorted by their father and mother, on their way to a weekend out of town.

This visit is high adventure for children, fraught with anticipation and some trepidation, particularly if it is the first time they have slept overnight away from familiar beds and their parents. They have their own suitcases, which they have packed and repacked several times during the day with pajamas, extra clothes, a book for bedtime, a favorite toy and a familiar cuddly creature. Even if the children have done this before, they are stimulated by going away. Its emotional impact on them is similar to the impact of a transcontinental flight on a grown-up.

None of this is new to you, grandparents. You have brought up your own kids and you know what they were like. The detailed advice in this chapter is not to teach you anything—think of it as a useful checklist for when the kids come to stay. Airplane pilots go through this kind of routine before takeoff.

Of course, you want your grandchildren to feel at home. Children may perhaps visit grandparents fairly often with their parents. If they are older and live not too far away the very best visits are when they drop in casually on their own. Each successive visit to the grandparents' house can have the appeal of exploring something already familiar and of being made comfortable in a home away from home. For the grandchild the house is new and exciting territory he is being invited to share. Our own grandchildren seem to know as much as we do about the details of things in our home and they are fascinated by things we take for granted. They love to poke around in our apartment spotting interesting objects and they do no harm.

One of our grandsons was visiting one day with a friend and took him on a tour, which we overheard: "This is the drawer where they keep their old-age tickets, and this is the telephone pad where they have the family numbers, their home and office numbers. Here is where the soft drinks, nuts and cookies are kept!"

We grandparents will be more totally involved when our grandchildren visit overnight or occasionally from a distance. If we have been out of touch with them for some time we will be tempted to overdo the hospitality. Remember, grandchildren want to come. Children are instinctively explorers and researchers who really want to know older people who belong to them. Let them know us as we are.

Before They Arrive

Don't go all out to put on a special show. It is nevertheless desirable to plan with forethought.

Prepare for a safe environment

When grandchildren visit and we are responsible for them, good preparations will make all of us more comfortable. While we don't need to restructure the whole house, we should get dangling wires out of harm's way, secure open doors leading to steep dark cellar stairs, and put away breakable objects. It is a good idea to put pills in bathroom cupboards out of reach, and do give some thought to the cleaning compounds in the utility cupboard.

On the positive side, we can provide special boxes of play materials, perhaps provided by the parents or at least suggested by them. Yes, do ask the parents ahead of time for suggestions about the kind of toys to provide. We can offer the grandchildren some drawers to explore in, but do not think for a moment that they will not get into other drawers. Margaret Kidd, a leader in early childhood education, said: "The Boy Scouts had a phrase for it, be prepared! It's quite a challenge to match the toy or book or puzzle with the particular child's interest. Sometimes beautiful household junk is more intriguing to preschoolers than educational toys. But one has to know the child. It's like choosing the perfect birthday gift. It has to be right for the person involved." Old hats, scarves, curtains, tins (with no sharp edges) and spoons can be just right. If your grandchildren visit frequently, you might consider asking the parents to leave some of their favorite puzzles or books with you for them to rediscover on subsequent visits.

Toybox and Fridge

A child's extended visit (a day or more) to grandparents requires preparation at both ends. Parents need to bring or send the necessary changes of clothing, special foods, bottles and comfort toys. Special arrangements by grandparents are crucial, for example, borrowing a crib or fixing a bed securely. What about a high chair and a car seat? Remember to buy groceries with their special needs in mind, and do your big shopping ahead of time; your time will be filled after their arrival. Dig out children's books, play materials or records; arrange for safe play spaces; retrieve games and avocational interests saved to share with grandchildren. If you indulge in painting and clay play, these materials may need some preparation. If you are talking to the family on the telephone before a planned visit, you could ask your grandchildren what they would like to do when they come and what they would like to bring with them to Granny's house.

Discuss with parents ahead of time acceptable discipline, bed times, their habits concerning food and sleep. Do they get picked up in the night? Remember to ask about special likes, dislikes and fears.

Telephone Numbers

Be sure that the parents leave telephone numbers where they can be reached. Grandparents also need to keep on hand a list of emergency numbers (doctor, fire, hospital, poison center). What age is at greatest risk during an emergency? Children younger than six months of age. If you think your grandchildren are in trouble, for example if there are continued loose bowel movements or vomiting, phone the doctor or the emergency number of the hospital.

Day One

Separation

If visiting involves being left at Granddad's place without Mother or Father, a sense of loss or desertion may need to be dealt with, commonly called homesickness. Parents should prepare children by discussing this with them, and grandparents have to face it when the parents are not there. Though the parents should allow time for the moment of separation, they should not turn the leave-taking into a demonstration that their children love them. Depending on the child's age, the emotional pull can be very strong. He will need reassurance from Mommy and Daddy that they will return. A baby or toddler can be diverted with a toy or a project to avoid prolonging the tensions. These displays should not hurt our feelings. They are the natural emotions of a strong child-parent attachment. Get on with the parting and, wonder of wonders, more often than not the visiting children will settle right down, though they may still miss Mommy at bedtime.

Familiarization

Take time to make your place familiar to visiting children. Make sure they know where things are, beds, switches, bathroom and so forth. Show them some attractive places to play and explore. You will be spending a lot of time in the kitchen, so talk to them about helping you with cooking, which may involve a lot of sink play. You have time for it, and Mother may not. They will remember the things you do together during the visit. Be sure to consult them about what they want to do; don't just serve up your bag of tricks.

It is perfectly all right to have some rules, like, "We can't let you use the hi-fi by yourself." They need time alone and so do you, so do not try to entertain them continuously. You can tell them when it is time for quiet play and when it is rest time for them as well as you. Let them be aware of your rhythms, your limits, your patterns of life. Balance their scheduled needs with yours.

The Visit Progresses

Space

Grandparents who are retired couples tend to spend a lot of time together at home. In our own case my husband cooks a few special things, and I keep out of the way. He makes a pass at cleaning up afterward, and he knows that I avoid complaining about the bits he misses. When couples are by themselves they find ways to accommodate the need for space, sometimes by planning and sometimes just by the way they evolve their daily rounds of activities. These things are a natural part of a continuing love affair. My husband and I want access to the computer at which we both work, but the competition usually resolves itself because neither of us works all day. We have adapted to close quarters and extended time together, but the equation changes when even one grandchild joins the crowd.

When grandchildren come for an extended visit, someone may start to suffer from "clusterphobia." We grandparents are usually so pleased to have our grandchildren that we reach for accommodation. One grandfather gave up trying to cope within the walls of his apartment. He and the grandchildren opened a pretend store in the apartment party room downstairs. They brought down empty cartons and cans, wooden spoons, paper bags and play money, and he and his grandchildren played at storekeeping. It was so successful that the children demanded repeat performances.

Be available

Being relaxed and available is hard to do sometimes, but it pays off. Your grandchildren become more creative; and there is more enjoyment and more appreciation. You can make a playhouse by throwing a blanket over the dining-room table. Another solution to the space problem is to use the out-of-doors as much as possible: walks and excursions and an occasional meal out.

They are visiting you, and you should remember that you are the star attraction. You are why they have come. Though you are the center of their attention, you'll do best not to smother or overwhelm them. In arranging the day for the things you do together, you are planning to make yourself available to them so that they have a chance to know you better. This latter is the aspect of their visit they appreciate most and will remember longest. You will usually find they reciprocate with openness and spontaneity.

You're special

You should try to be aware of your own capacities and limits. All of us know how we are with children because we have brought up our own. Some of us have dealt with many children in large families or as teachers in schools. Some grandparents are more sensitive than others to children's needs. Honest differences of these kinds can be recognized and balanced. Some grandparents have a skill in carpentry, for example, or skiing, playing ball, theater, music, dance, outdoor crafts, gardening or science. Some are storytellers, some walkers or talkers. Some enjoy movies more than others. Some are cuddly, others more verbal, still others more silently companionable. These differences are not a problem for children, as long as we remain open and warm.

Correspondents

I have corresponded with a number of grandparents about what went on when their grandchildren visited; several of their accounts follow. They have shared their experiences in the hope that they may stimulate other ideas. Modern grandparents who live without much contact with children may wonder in advance whether they can adequately meet the children's needs. One grandmother said to me, "They get bored at my house. They have so many toys at their own house I feel I have to take them places or they won't have any fun." She appreciated talking to other grandmothers and claimed she got a lot of new ideas from them. Out of her own experience she inspired some other grandparents to take their grandchildren to special art classes and on boat trips. Grandparents are not necessarily child-care specialists, but they can take the children to creative programs at art galleries, children's drop-in centers, libraries and parks.

Don't let television take over

Sometimes it is easier, with modern conveniences and instant entertainment—television and VCRs—to let the more personal aspects of grandparenting opportunities slip. The role of television as a baby-sitter is both appreciated and abused. We need a family discussion with all parties involved to determine the use of this magic tool. We need to insert some judgment of our own when we're in charge.

One grandmother, Sally, wrote me an amusing letter about this: "During a visit from our six-year-old grandson, he asked to be allowed to delay bedtime for one more hour to watch a TV program he had often been permitted to watch at home. Toward the end of the hour we noticed that he had dozed off and suggested that he turn off the TV and go to bed. Sleepy and caught off gaurd, he pleaded for a few more minutes so he could see the denouement, which he described in some detail. Said exasperated Grandfather, 'Do you mean that this is a rerun of a program you've already seen?' 'Yes,' he said, 'but I'm a fast forgetter.'"

Grandma Alice said, "I find it hard to suggest simple things like reading to them or playing games when I think they'd prefer TV. But I wonder. Maybe they would like the feeling that I care enough to want to *do* something with them." Helping grandparents with necessary jobs can be surprisingly satisfying to children, and they enjoy jobs such as making beds, putting out the garbage, setting the table, shopping, putting groceries away, making a milk shake, cutting up apples, rolling pie crust and making peanut-butter sandwiches and many more practical activities working alongside us.

June writes: "Books have always been a favorite pastime for me and my grandchildren. I love to read to them. Stories lead to discussions and quite often can settle problems or set examples."

"My one day a week with baby Fiona—how I love it!" said Grandma Rose when I met her at the grocery store. "It's my day off from work." Fiona is deposited at 8:00 A.M. and picked up at 7:00 P.M. As I observed the two of them, Rose was talking with Fiona, age eighteen months. They were naming and choosing some grocery items. Fiona was speaking fluently: "What's that, beans? I like 'sparagrass, too." Rose's eyes were sparkling.

"We always had plenty to do at our grandparents' house," said Nathan, as he thought back to younger days when he and his brother visited their grandparents. "In their big backyard Grandpa would show us how to cast. He was sure his grandsons would become good fishermen. We did really go fishing with him sometimes, but even in the backyard he would cut two poles and without lines or hooks we would practice the cast. The ravine behind their house was a perfect place to climb and dig and play with cars and trucks. Lunchtime was fun, too. We each had a tray to carry out to the backyard. We ate under the trees at a picnic table. And then there was the attic. What treasures we dug up there!"

Grandma Bronwyn writes about going to the movies occasionally when the grandchildren come visiting: "The grandchildren take *us* to the movies because of Grandpa Ben's special handicap. He is in a wheelchair. It takes two to push the wheelchair. I love the memory of the day our fourteen- and sixteen-year-old granddaughters tooks us to see *Crocodile Dundee.* As Jill pushed the wheelchair Sarah went ahead and located seats. Suddenly in the dark came a shout—I'm losing him, Granny, I'm losing him! Ben came racing towards me down the slope with Jill falling to her knees trying to hold the wheels back. On went the lights, up rushed the ushers and order was restored. Great memories of that panic we recall together, and we smile with relief that we survived together. We enjoy their visits!"

Grandma Elaine writes: "There used to be a pattern to grandchildren's visits. They usually came on weekends, and their father often retired for an afternoon sleep or to watch football on TV while the rest of us, being more active, would go for a walk to various favorite places—like the railway station where there is a steam engine preserved, or wood trails with lots of opportunities of playing camouflage, a variation of hide-and-seek, where the child is entirely visible but the adults pretend not to notice because of the clever camouflage. After dinner the special event was a play or concert put on by the two boys and rehearsed in private while the adults had their predinner drinks. That was probably the highlight of the visit for them."

Elaine continued, "Our grandchildren have always enjoyed working on real jobs and helping on projects like building a dock, raking leaves, making wooden models from scratch with Grandpa, but always as equal partners, not just observers."

My own vivid memories of grandparents pertain more to their personal qualities than to particular things we did. My grandfather was stern and remote. He must have felt he could talk more intelligently with my brother, and he certainly favored him. The granddaughters in our large family felt isolated from Grandfather. He had been brought up in a family with six sisters, and that may have seemed to him to be enough young girls for a lifetime.

Grandmother saved the day for us. She was never at a loss to involve us in household chores, making us feel needed and appreciated. She did a great deal of needlework and taught us some of these skills. She made all her birthday and Christmas presents, and we learned a few of her arts. As we worked together, talk was constant—we had so much to tell each other, and time for it. Perhaps this is the difference between a generation ago and today. Having enough time is a precious part of good relations with children, and modern grandparents need to work on establishing time.

Share

Another way to enjoy grandchildren is to share your friends with them. Sometimes friends can do special projects with them that you cannot—take them out in a boat, for example, or show them a special skill or something of historical interest. Sometimes your friends are interesting in themselves, but your grandchildren will not thank you for saddling them with friends they think are bores. Children seldom find other young people boring. If you know some of them who are sufficiently responsible and experienced, you can ask them to look after your grandchildren for a specified time. This is one good way to involve your grandchildren with some vigorous play.

Bedtime, television, manners

The struggle of bedtime and lights out can be handled a little more leniently at Grandma's house than at the grandchildren's house. The routine is not as firmly established as at home, when bedtime ceremonies are often essential routines. You may be asked to incorporate some of the ceremonies, such as bedtime snack, story, a final tape, a little reading before lights out. When a child responds negatively to, "It's time for bed," one way of handling it, which usually works, is to say "Okay, this *is* your bedtime, but you can read in bed for a while if you like." This provides him with a good self-directed impetus and will probably induce relaxation so that sleep takes over before reading goes on too long. In other words, a small reward often deadens the pain of having to accept a disciplined fact. Simon, my twelve-year-old grandson, says: "But if you let them go on for as long as they like, they can get away with anything!" He is right. There is always the bookworm you need to check on, so reading doesn't go on all night!

Concerning TV, the above formula is no good, because most TV is stimulating rather than relaxing for children before bed. "More, more," is the recurring cry. Television must be regulated if children are to enjoy other activities such as talking, reading and playing. Time for creativity, original enterprise and physical activity is precious time and should not be circumvented by overindulging in TV. Discriminate between using TV as a time filler and choosing television that's worth watching.

Grandparents are often caught short by a grandchild who says: "But my mommy always lets me watch that." The more you know about programs they are allowed to watch the clearer you can be with your discipline. If you don't have a clue, offer a time limitation with a reward at the end, perhaps playing some popular game.

As to manners: one Ottawa grandmother was puzzled about how to develop better table manners in her grandchildren who come to visit her from New York two or three times a year. After much thought she decided to speak to their parents, suggesting that it might be appropriate for them to ask their children to observe and try to use the kind of table manners their grandparents used while visiting in the grandparents' house. Well, it worked. And it helped the parents raise their standards of table manners, too. Parents can be forgiven for not stressing table manners in the interest of getting a problem child to enjoy eating, but this subtle approach benefitted everyone in the long run.

Coping with Problems

Withdrawal Symptoms

All of us have had experience in dealing with this. We expect spontaneity on the part of the child and suddenly it is not there. We ask questions, and the answers are unenthusiastic and short. Appetites drop, and there is an air of boredom. We can be sure the negative behavior is saying something, and we should try first to understand the causes. The symptoms may indicate a reaction against our household or us, or they may be caused by something else. The difficulty is that a child may be unable or unwilling to confide in us at the time of our choosing. And we may be too polite to ask our grandchildren: "What gives?" The parents may already have the explanation: something psychological, something wrong at school or some physical condition to be followed up with the family doctor. We should ask them.

Grandparents have had many years of experience with emotional scenes. We can be flexible. Withdrawal from meals may be resolved by rescheduling mealtimes or presenting them in a simpler way. (Check behavior expectations in Chapter

Three.) Withdrawal or temper tantrums may indicate deeper uncertainties that need more attention. Grandparents should refer major behavior problems to the parents.

Relations between parents and grandchild may have been going through a patch of tension, probably temporary. But your grandchild may arrive at your house ready to take out his woes on his grandparents. This situation may be difficult, but grandparents can pick their course with patience and delicacy, careful not to act as a proxy for the parent unless asked to do so and not adding to the child's troubles by prying. The parents should be told what you are seeing and what you think about it. They will handle it in their own time. The parents may not yet be in the market for advice from us.

Grandma Su had been experiencing her grandson's unusual shyness. Then suddenly she was faced with Freddie's question: "Can I stay at your house all the time?" Her grandson's father was a single parent and doing his best, but the grandson was looking for something better. There is of course a possibility, a dangerous one, that the question might have been prompted by the grandmother exploiting an emotionally fragile relationship between the child and his father. In this case, I do not think so. In any event Su tossed the question around in her mind for a while. She lived alone and taught nursery school. She could work it out if Freddie and his father both wanted it. Then she thought: "I like being a grandparent. I have twelve grandchildren and I have no desire to be a parent again unless there is no alternative." She hugged Freddie and said. "You come and visit me just as often as you can and stay overnight sometimes but not every day. I love you, Freddie."

When They Run Off

It is of course a serious matter if a child disappears, and grandparents should give thought in advance to what they would do. The parents may or may not be quickly available. There may or may not be some neighbors to help in a quick search. There is a point at which the police should be called, and how long to wait depends to some extent on the circumstances, such as where you live and how old the child is. Best of all, of course, is prevention, meaning keeping your eye on your grandchild, preparing safe play space for younger ones and making agreements with older children. Safety, of course, is the bottom line. If a grandchild is not safe nothing else matters.

Some discussion of the question of getting lost might be a fine precautionary plan. With little ones, getting lost in a store is a possibility. Suggest: 1) they should stay close to you so you'll know where they are; 2) if they get lost they should call out your name, not just yell "Grandma"; 3) they should ask someone behind the counter to help rather than ask a stranger. And they shouldn't hide. Explain that if they are really lost the lady or man behind the counter might take them to the lost and found, and you would go there and find them.

It often turns out that older children lose track of time or wander out of sight. Helen told me, with some emotion, of how she took her eleven-year-old twin grandchildren to the neighborhood park in Vancouver. She suggested the territorial limitations of their exploration and said, "We'll meet in half an hour at the big maple tree." They were not back at the appointed place, and half an hour grew to three quarters of an hour. After what seemed an eternity they turned up smiling, "Oh, Grandma, we had such a good time playing Pooh sticks in the stream we forgot about the time." Helen said she would lend them her watch next time and explained how worried she had been and how keeping promises was important.

On special excursions grandchildren should not be left alone in areas that might involve danger or where they might get lost. There is a fine line between risk and judgment. To err on the cautionary side is usually wise, but there are times to recognize maturity. It took great confidence on my part to let my grandson David, fifteen, go back through the crowd for quite a long distance to find his camera, which he had left behind at the huge baseball stadium. Brother Peter, ten, kept assuring me that David would find it and come back safe and sound to the spot we had agreed on. Back he came, with his camera, after twenty uneasy minutes for Grandma.

Discipline

Parents frequently complain that grandparents do not support their discipline when their children visit the grandparents. Grandparents may be more lenient with their grandchildren because they feel the children have been overdisciplined, but we should not abuse our privilege, and we certainly should not risk a child's health or welfare by being overindulgent. Discipline can be clearly understood by a child of she is given respect and if her point of view is taken into account. Spanking and slapping are adult power tools that produce obedience, perhaps, but not much cooperation or appreciation. (See Chapter Three.)

Much discipline was formerly and still is based on obedience with the threat of physical punishment—the kind that gives all rights to the elders and mere subservience to children. If that's the way you want it, you are in for rebellion and disrespect with the likelihood that the children will decide to leave home (or grandparents' home) as soon as they possibly can. People don't like being trodden on. And children are people!

A much better approach, when siblings are fighting and one is blaming the other for starting it, would be for a grandparent to say: "I don't care who started the fighting, what can we do about it?" Just as in the case of driving in the car when fighting erupts, get the children to make suggestions about solving the problem. They may suggest a time out, or say, "Let's have lunch".

Growing toward Self-discipline

Helping youngsters acquire self-discipline is the goal of any grandparent's or parent's discipline. The whole point of involving the child in discussions of acceptable behavior and of values is to allow him to develop a standard of behavior that he feels good about, that he can depend upon and that he can evaluate with others in the process of his maturing. If the discipline is all done *for* him, he will feel free to chuck it and use an adopted set of principles that might make him more dependent on other people's morals than on his own best judgment. If we keep this in mind when he is visiting with us, we will find our task more enjoyable.

Self-adopted discipline comes more naturally to children who have been brought up in a democratic atmosphere, having had a share in decision making and in setting the rules and a chance, as one teenager said, to make some gorgeous mistakes. In the development toward adulthood there is much insecurity, trial and error and mirror gazing. Grandparents sometimes confuse a young person's contemplation of risk with the reality of proceeding with dangerous behavior.

The telephone

The use of the telephone is an example of the teenager's need to explore exciting and daring ideas. When grandchildren visit grandparents, they may have to have some brakes put on them in the use of the telephone if it becomes too intrusive. However, if you can put up with a little disturbance, it just might be a grandchild's only chance to carry on a very important conversation with a friend without the listening ears of siblings and parents. "Grandma's house has a perfect phone in the basement," said Barbie, fourteen. "I'll call you from there later, Bob." Private talk can be confidence-building, a sheltered sharing of ideas before personal confrontation. It's all part of sorting out "Who am I?" "What do we think?" and "Where are we going?" Grandparents who allow adolescents privacy are often rewarded with confidences.

Siblings

When more than one grandchild visits, sibling rivalry may disturb the peace from time to time. It may take the form of vying for a grandparent's attention—"It's my turn to play that game with Grandpa." Perhaps Grandpa can handle it by saying: "I'll play one game with you, Bobby, and then I'll play one game with Anna." But it may not be that simple. A rumpus may be an expression of vim and vigor, perhaps needing no intervention but possibly showing a need for more space to exercise some muscles. Boisterous play can include anger, teasing and hitting, and children can get hurt.

When cousins from a distance get together at grandparents' house there is a limit to the amount of boisterous free play that can be tolerated. There comes a time when planning is imperative. Four of our grandchildren had a reunion with us for a few days on their way to summer camp. Roughhouse developed from time to time. Sibling rivalry, cousinly rivalry and just sheer exuberance required some guidance. An adult needed to be on hand to lend support to an insecure swimmer and to remind the gang of consideration and pool etiquette. They had to be discouraged from throwing paper darts and perhaps heavier objects from our high outdoor deck.

Grandparents need to have some artful dodges at hand as they sense the oncoming of destructive play. A few suggestions follow.

Recognize the situation. "This play is getting too rough; somebody may get hurt." And then, with the grandchildren's help, make a list of things to do in the next hour before dinner: read, help with preparing dinner, draw a picture, write a letter, listen to music.

If the children need separating, one of them can be given a chance to try out some special "adult" game and the other the privilege of working on a special project in the kitchen where, incidentally, Grandma might have the chance for a tête à tête.

Ordering them to play nicely can create resentments. An older sibling may have had too much responsibility thrust upon him and resent being told to look after his little sister who may feel, in her turn, that she is being thrown to the wolves. This is a point at which to introduce alternative activities. By giving special recognition to the underlying rivalries we may be able to produce surprisingly positive results. Remember to say so at some later time, "You were wonderful to have as visitors."

The love-hate relationship between siblings is a natural phenomenon. It stems from competition and rivalry over their parents' love, from inferiority feelings and unfair disciplinary practices. Some siblings gang up on one another. Some are more sensitively attuned to a brother or a sister. Deep and important feelings can get expressed at the grandparents' house. Rather than resenting the strong feelings, grandparents might consider themselves lucky to be trusted with such emotions. Sibling rivalry cannot be removed but it can be redirected.

Sibling relations are not always negative. It is great to have a big brother stand up for you when you tangle with a bully. A little sister who dotes on cuddly stuffed animals is not all wrong in her brother's eyes. Jane's brother gave Grandma a hint for a Christmas gift: "She'd love one of those Santa bears," he said with a twinkle in his eye.

My older brother, Jim, was capable of giving me a hard time. He once told me: "Dolls don't have feelings, Sis." I replied with something like, "All except Joey." (Joey was my doll.) He agreed. This must have been a high point of our relationship, because I remember it. Jim wanted to tease me for being too sentimental with my dolls, but he respected the feeling I had for Joey.

Evidence of basic respect among siblings came to us in the story of Peter (age ten). He was interested in the peace marches that had been going on in his community in California. He dreamed of going to the final day of the big Peace Walk in Washington, D.C. One of his grandmothers lived in Washington, and he thought it would be easy to arrange a visit. But it was not easy physically or financially.

His older sister, Victoria, was at college and happened to hear that a friend was going to the Peace March. She alerted the family. Peter traveled to Washington with the friend and stayed with his grandmother. Various members of the family chipped in to help finance the trip, including a contribution from his brother David out of earnings from his part-time job. Incidentally, Peter's Washington grandmother accompanied him on the march.

One at a Time

Many grandparents reach the conclusion that it is best to have grandchildren visit one at a time. "Total immersion," having a direct relationship with a grandchild for a period of time, all by herself, without her parents or siblings, is a good way to get to know her. Grandma Karen from South Carolina writes: "I enjoy trying to provide special times with my older grandchildren, one by one, such as the theater, dining at a nice restaurant and the ballet."

Grandma Charlotte in Ottawa: "I paint pictures with my fourteen-year-old granddaughter, and we drink tea and eat cookies, which she bakes. I am not a threat as a cook to either of my daughters-in-law or granddaughters, which causes a lot of merriment and extra love to be sure my feelings are not hurt. My tall thirteen-year-old grandson comes over and helps me do things I am too old to do and becomes quite bossy. 'I'll go up the ladder. You stay off it. What would I tell my dad if you fell off it?'"

Visiting at our house may not always be easy but it helps grandchildren to establish a sense of their own roots. It is even more important in broken families to strengthen intergenerational bonds wherever possible. In the midst of some of the changes and confusions of new family relationships, we can anchor one set of connections.

9

Grandparents Visit Grandchildren

In the previous chapter the stage setting was our own home. Here we take the show on the road to perform in their own home. Visiting grandchildren in their own homes is easier on the whole because we can usually expect the parents to do most of the work, at least when they are there. The cast of stars is the same, and so is the psychology. Problems do arise, however, problems that will be less severe if they are foreseen.

Our grandchildren's lives are rooted in their house. Their territories are familiar to them. It is the best place to see them in a relaxed setting, doing what comes naturally in the routine of their lives. Our expectations of their family life, however, may be quite different from the reality. Whether we arrive from a distance or live nearby, we enter into another family's living patterns, and this may create some hurdles for us. We have our own rigidities and prejudice (right or wrong) about the way to do things and we face a young family whose life-style may be unlike anything we knew in our day. If divorce, single parenting or remarriage is involved as well, we may bring additional trepidations and emotional hang-ups with us.

In all probability *our* household (where our son or daughter was brought up) was very different than theirs. It is important to keep in mind that we evolved our ideas about how to do things in that earlier household, and that it was the best arrangement we could manage. It may, however, have become an outdated pattern by now.

This brings us to guilt feelings. If any grandparents do not regret mistakes they made as parents, will they please stand up? None of us stand—at least that point is settled. Memories of where we went wrong can easily disturb us. We may have been too strict or too lenient. However, although we made mistakes, we are entitled to forgive ourselves now. Past errors need not lead to a life sentence.

The Visit Itself

Our adjustment to our child's home will be less difficult if we arrive rested and if we are warmly anticipated. It is important to enter as freely as possible into their environment, ready to take it on its merits. Nothing is difficult if we can regard each day as a good day, carry little baggage from the past and look forward to opportunities to share enjoyment.

It also helps if we plan the details of our arrival and our stay so they cause minimal disruption to the household, perhaps arriving on a weekend instead of a weekday. It is always better for a visit to be too short than too long and far better for everyone to feel they wish it could have lasted longer.

We will arrive with more confidence if we are lucky enough to be in frequent communication with the family. Even so, their schedules may be such as to imbue any grandparent with a certain feeling of disorientation. To be in a contemporary house, where neither father nor mother arrives home from work till nearly six, can be a taxing experience for grandparents. Mother has stopped to pick up her youngest at his day-care center and his older sister at her after-school program. Father brings an armful of groceries. As they pour into the house and greet the grandparents, the children watch TV and the father hurries to prepare the evening meal. It is understandable if a grandparent experiences culture shock on first exposure.

Housekeeping

Our adult children may look forward to our visit with anticipation or with trepidation. They may see us as guests to be catered to or as family who can look after themselves. They may have gone out of their way to have everything ready and polished for our arrival, or they may expect us to make up the guest bed and dig in with dinner preparations. We grandparents do recoil a bit if the house isn't clean, the guest and bathroom towels aren't ready, and the meals are ultra casual. But pointing out that things don't meet our expectations isn't likely to help.

Neither is comparing a sister or sister-in-law's more artful ways of receiving and entertaining us! (And remember these days that a son or son-in-law is just as responsible for housekeeping responsibilities.) The truth is that grandparents will not be as welcome as they want to be unless they can take the household as it is and avoid imposing extra stress on pressed parents.

Ask your children to be frank in discussing the state of the house and the arrangements they have made. Explain that you are hesitant to clear up a pile of children's clothes or to change the towels unless you are confident that the parents will not take these actions as implied criticism of their housekeeping.

Now to the purpose of our visit and how to make the most of it!

Focus on the Children

When we visit our grandchildren for long or for short visits, we can be sure *they* would like to be the focus of attention. Some grandparents achieve this result easily. They are direct and warm (whether or not they come bearing gifts) and the children feel they are important to them. When we unthinkingly slip into adult-only conversation, we must appear to our grandchildren to want to chat more about the parents' doings than about theirs. Of course, there are many occasions when a visit to our grandchildren's house is a brief visit. These are often precious times when we have to catch up on important matters, but we may be in danger of neglecting our grandchildren and spending too much time with our adult children.

This does not mean that grandparents should overwhelm the grandchildren with hugs and gifts and hover over them. That only builds expectations, some resistance and false notions of who and what grandparents are. We establish good relationships when we include grandchildren in our conversation and spend some time with them. This is their house, their playground. They want to show us and tell us about their recent accomplishments and we should, if we have the opportunity, take time to get to know them better in this setting.

Billy was overheard to say to a friend: "My grandmother's nice when I talk to her on the phone. She's always wondering what I've been doing and says she wants to see me. But when she comes to our house all she does is talk to Mom. And Grandpa and Dad talk all the time about politics and business. I was hoping Grandpa would show me some of those neat tricks he does with string." To paraphrase: I thought they wanted to see me and talk to me, but I guess they think I'm not grown up enough yet.

On the other hand an overload of attention to grandchildren can be uncomfortable for the children and intrusive. Sarah writes about her co-grandparents. She calls them "the other grandparents"! She feels they are too possessive and that they visit too often. "*We* feel that it is important not to overdo it, not to impose on the time of children and grandchildren. *We* think that grandchildren need breathing room to develop under their parents' guidance and care without the constant interference of loving grandparents." She thinks the other grandparents feel competitive, that they seem to need more time with the children and that they coddle them like babies, which they no longer are.

Links with Our Past

Identifying objects and pictures in their house that relate to *our* family history intrigues grandchildren. A conversation might go like this: "That picture on the dining-room wall shows the lake and our old boathouse where your daddy played when he was a little boy." Or, "The rug on your hall floor comes from Africa. Grandpa brought it back with him when he went there on a mission for the World Bank." With any luck your grandchild will ask, "What's a mission? What's the World Bank?" or "Where's Africa?" and then you have a chance to show him a map and tell him a story. Or a chat might go: "When your mommy was growing up we used those snowshoes over your mantel to tramp around in the country. Of course we skiied a lot then, too, just like you do today. Let's go and have a look at your new skis and you can tell me your plans for skiing this winter."

When Helpers Need Help

Gadgetry in the households of young families demands more attention than it used to. Our grandchildren often know more than we grandparents do about how to work the new tape recorder, the oven or the house thermostat. Older children tend to "take over" to show us how things work. However, the kids may not know *all* the answers, and grandparents would do well to get clued in to the new machines as part of our introduction to the household.

The novelty of our children's homes does not always make our "helping hands," though offered willingly, as effective as we would wish. I will never forget the special problems that developed forty years ago when my mother came some distance to help out following two broken bones in our family. Grandma Katie, after struggling with our setup for a week, coping with unaccustomed floor levels and a cantankerous washing machine, was managing nicely when she slipped on the basement floor and fractured her collarbone!

The unfamiliar scene is part of the problem for visiting grandparents. Overanxious attitudes are another cause of insecurity. A few years ago, as the visiting grandmother of a six-year-old, I responded to her invitation to play soccer in the backyard. In a vigorous kick I skidded on a slippery place and fell on my elbow. Too enthusiastic a grandmother, I. Jane and I were alone at their house. I knew I had broken a bone (the elbow was swelling), and after Jane found the Aspirin box (bless her heart) I phoned the hospital to inquire about entrance procedures for the emergency department. While we waited for my husband and Jane's brother Simon to come home from Simon's hockey game with the car, we talked about the details of how we would arrange the rest of the weekend visit. We phoned the parents, of course, although I hated to do so, since they were away on a ski weekend. Fortunately, it was near the end of the weekend and Grandpa said he could manage until they returned. I cogitated on the stupidity of one grandmother!

Health and Fitness of Grandparents

Problems of grandparent's physical fitness and health can become heightened in our children's houses. If there are such problems they should be shared with the parents and, where appropriate, with the grandchildren. We can function better if we are frank about such things. The challenge is to know our limits and to temper the extremes of physical effort. Steep stairs and allergy-provoking cats may be among the hurdles.

Trips with grandchildren to the zoo or the museum are wonderful opportunities and can be great fun if our grandchildren modulate the pace to suit the grandparents. Grandchildren can quickly become aware of our less agile bodies and can be sensitive to our needs for help occasionally.

The Neighborhood

The neighborhood has an important bearing on family life. If our grandchildren live in strip suburbia, we may be struck by its limitations; it is less human than neighborhoods used to be. People depend on their cars instead of walking, and we discover in taking a walk around the neighborhood with our grandchildren that nobody's out on the street! Backyards are manicured, tidy and unused. They don't have as much good junk in them as they used to. In my husband's grandfather's backyard, there was a rusty railway handcar the old man had used to pump his way out to the family cottage every Friday night, with special leave from the CPR. I wish our youngsters could have more good junk like that around to interest them and arouse their imaginations.

Even if there's no old junk around, we grandparents may be able to find some alternative activities in excursions to old houses or houses that are just being built. Some recreation programs provide areas for creative play with old dress-up materials and props. And then there are heritage excursions.

Cities pose other problems. The prevalence of crime has led many parents and grandparents to organize block associations for supervision and safe houses. There are programs to street proof kids, teaching them such things as not to get into cars with strangers. When we visit we need to know about the dangers and the safeguards.

Environment

The natural environment has been abused, and our grandchildren and their children are the ones who will suffer from its destruction. Management of the environment is going to get more attention in future. Even though grandparents and grandchildren are unlikely to spend much time talking about the ozone layer, many aspects of the environment are important and can be used to foster relationships with grandchildren and help them understand its importance. Children will always remember what they learn with their grandparents about flowers, birds and nature lore. In the cities they are accustomed to dogs and cats, but few other animals; even horses are rare. Grandparents are old enough to have enjoyed easier access to countryside and to farms and may be the only access their grandchildren have to this rural way of life. We can recreate for our grandchildren our connection to these resources by taking them to orchards, to collect brush, to cut Christmas trees or to visit petting zoos.

Outside activities

Grandchildren's programs of outside activities can bewilder grandparents. Children often go off to hockey practices, music lessons and other appointments after school. Plans for hockey practices, music lessons or sleep overs should be part of a grandparent's preparation. Similarly, if you have plans for very special excursions with your grandchildren, such as a boat ride, a visit to an amusement park, a hay ride or a picnic on the beach, you should alert the parents and your grandchildren of such plans.

What To Do When You Visit

Grandma Elaine says her visits to her grandchildren often occurred when one or another child was sick or the parents were away. If the children were well, their rituals included a walk with Grandpa, when they would pretend to have gone too far and were reduced to eating their shoelaces! With Grandma it was a story in bed early in the morning before they had to get up for breakfast. Rituals are remembered with joy, and the grandchildren ask for repeat performances.

Sally had a clue to getting along with her grandchildren at their house when she was looking after them. Let them help with the cooking, she suggested. Ask them to tell you their favorite foods and you share some of your "specials" with them. They probably know where things are kept better than you do. It will, of course, take more time sharing the cooking, but these experiences make for wonderful memories. "Do you remember when we made scrambled eggs together?" fifteen-year-old Josh asked his grandmother years later. He said: "You know, I made applesauce last week just like the kind you and I used to make when I was little."

Ask your daughter or son what they remember and liked best about their grandparents' visits. Take some clues from them. Grandma Maria said she asked her son that question and got this answer: "They talked to me as if I was somebody and not just a child. What I really liked best, as we played around the kitchen, was to hear the stories of your childhood, and I liked making chocolate cake with Grandma, too." Maria grew up in Italy in a family of ten children. She was the eldest child and came by child-tending and cooking naturally.

Birthdays

Chocolate cake reminds me of birthday parties. We grandparents are often asked to our grandchildren's birthday parties. We may bake a traditional birthday cake and take it with us. Or one of the parents may be well up on birthday cakes and enjoy making them with the children.

One birthday party model that lasted successfully for us for several years was an outdoor party with borrowed painting easels and colored dough to work at and mold at tables in the backyard. The weather usually cooperated, as I recall, and of course we had the usual balloons and goodies to top up the afternoon. Children seemed to love our parties, and they were the kind that grandparents could easily help with and enjoy themselves at.

Some Dos and Don'ts for Visiting Grandparents

Don't try to be perfect. Relax and enjoy your visit. Some grandparents, like some parents, are especially good with babies or toddlers, some with young school-age children and some with teenagers. Grandparent perfection is impossible, and anyway it is undesirable; grandchildren would rather see you laugh and give them a chance to laugh back.

Don't try to change your routines completely to fit your grandchildren's. Let them see your rhythm and patterns of daily life.

Don't use a means of discipline that you know the parents reject. Support the parents' discipline. What do you do when you disapprove of the handling of discipline in your children's home? Save your comments for leisurely conversation. (If you can find such a time!) Discuss the issue in general. Take it easy. It's their home, their lives. Emphasize the positive.

Don't give more time than you have. Grandma Carli was asked to give two days a week to her grandchildren, ages two and four, on a regular basis. Mother worked and needed help and assumed that Grandmother would *love* to do it. It was too much for her. Give as much time as you feel like, and feel good about it.

Do have fun.

Do spend as much time as you can with your grandchildren.

Do listen to them talk, talk to them, play with them.

Grandparent in Charge

Sometimes we are asked to take charge in the children's home. This can take some practice. When both parents work, the pace of their household will be faster than we are used to, and the children will be used to living by timetables. The shopping probably has been done in bulk in a limited time slot. Planning meals around all this food takes some organization, especially if we are on our own with the children. Finding our way through the uncertainties of where everything is kept causes slowdowns. Serving meals at a time that fits children's needs is demanding. "I must finish supper by six-fifteen" said Billy. "I have homework to do and I want to watch TV at seven." The pace feels faster. Of course, we may be slower.

Following our basic adjustment to our children's household, we may confront a few more questions. How much TV should the children watch? When and where should we let the dog out, and who is in charge of him? Clearance with the parents on these issues is a must.

Sometimes a grandparent who is in charge while the parents are away gets caught up in a grandchild's worries. Albert, age ten, came home from school in an unusually sober mood. Grandma Mary was at his house preparing dinner. He did not talk about his trouble for a while, but finally it came out. He had been playing touch football in the school yard and had tripped one of the players, who blasted him with threats and swear words. "The guy is a bully," said Albert. "He fights hard." Albert was afraid to go to school the next day because of the threats. He and his grandma talked a while. Grandma was mainly a loving listening post while Albert sorted our his tangled feelings.

A common pressure that children feel, usually from their parents but sometimes from their grandparents, is the emphasis on doing well at school. We grandparents may say, "It's not your marks that count. It's how hard you work," but we tend to boast about their good grades. Children may feel that because the adults are so clever (at least in the children's eyes) they, too, should be smart. They can possibly spend too much energy trying to live up to parents' and grandparents' seeming expectations. We can encourage our grandchildren to feel satisfied and comfortable with their achievements and help them slacken the competitive pitch.

A nagging child is difficult for a grandparent. He can get on your nerves. Nagging and whining are attention-getting behavior. We might try to figure out what our grandchild really wants or needs by way of special attention. Why is he upset? It may have little to do with his whining words: "I want to go watch television" "Why can't we go now?" "Bobby hit me" "Will you buy me that?" His need for special attention might be disguising more important longings, such as, "I want my mommy," or, "Spend some of your precious time with me."

The burden of unhappy children makes for tension and worry. Complaining to the child about her whining only brings on more provocation. There are no easy prescriptions. But trying to find the source of the trouble makes sense. Is she jealous of a sibling? Is she still grieving over a personal loss? If you can guess the root cause (and we often can't) you will be able to proceed more confidently to give her the kind of attention that will help her feel she doesn't need to nag.

Day Care

One of the major factors, these days, for grandparents to take account of, when they visit their grandchildren, is the role day care, sitters or nannies play in the lives of their grandchildren and the differences they make in the children's home life. (We discussed the question of day care as a resource for family living in Chapter Six.) For some grandparents these new services have a profound effect on their relationships with grandchildren. Even though we grandparents are not as available as we used to be, we still like the honor of dropping in to see our precious grandchildren when we can. But often they're not there! What we need to realize is that, instead of being left with an untrained sitter or an older sibling (as happened very often in earlier years), they are in the hands of professionally trained child-care workers, and we should be thankful.

Day care is a major family resource rather than a "holding operation" as it is sometimes described. Some of the best educators have put their minds to early childhood education and understand the wonderful ways young children develop and participate in creative social learning. Health and security are prime ingredients of good day care, and basic to this facility is respect and concern for the individual child. Good staff people in this field are as fundamentally important as good teachers in the school system. The beginning years can build the foundations of inquiring minds, happiness and personal security.

Grandparents who find ways to meld day care's contribution to their grandchildren's lives with their own will be strengthened and rewarded with grandchildren who are socially well adjusted and who are eager to learn. Mind you, it has to be good day care.

The Rewards

Getting to know our grandchildren in their own environment has great advantages. The baby is more comfortable in his own crib and his carriage. His toys and equipment are familiar. The older children have their close friends and their pets at hand. Their routine with day care is established and we learn to fit into it.

The rewards of comfortable grandparenting come to us in subtle ways. One quiet afternoon, Grandmother Carli was looking after the children at her daughter's home because the regular sitter had to go to the dentist. She was talking to her twelve-year-old granddaughter, Anne, in a cozy corner of the kitchen while preparing dinner, when it all came out. "I had no idea," she said, "that so much feeling could be held inside such a little person. Anne told me, in a soft voice, 'Granny, I wish my mom could be home more. I really miss her when I come home from school. A sitter isn't the same as your mom.'" That was the beginning of some important communication between grandmother and granddaughter and between Carli and her daughter. It didn't result in the mother quitting her job, but it did encourage her to spend more special time with her daughter.

When grandparents visit grandchildren, the world can be full of delightful surprises. If we have been looking at some of the problem areas, it is only to clear the way for positive connections. Delightful surprises come in large and small packages: a puzzle solved, a ladder climbed, a painting admired, a book adored, a new friend, a lovely smile. What more can we ask?

10

Money and Grandparenting

The things we do are often attended by costs, and it is not surprising that grandparenting, too, raises questions of money. The best things are priceless, but in our society most things require the exchange of money. It costs something to travel to welcome the new baby, to choose a birthday present and to have the grandchildren for dinner.

Constraints

As grandparents we differ from one another in our tastes and personal values. A few grandparents are rich, many are poor, and the rest are in between. No matter what our incomes, big or small, they are less than we would like, and there are demands to be met aside from the needs of grandchildren. We have to weigh what we spend on them against all the other expenses we must meet.

There are some situations in which most grandparents would react in the same way. If a grandchild is deprived of something important to her welfare, there is not much question that we would give to the extent of our means. It may not be enough but we give it our best shot and, like the widow's mite, it means a lot.

In more ordinary circumstances, we face many questions when we wonder whether we can or should contribute to the young family. Most parents with children these days struggle to make ends meet. Grandparents may wonder whether they should give what they can to help even though they have similar problems themselves. These are delicate questions of balance with decisions for each individual to make.

Our married sons or daughters may always have been dependent on us for support. Or perhaps we made it clear at a certain stage that they were on their own; we had brought them up and seen them through their formal education, but now we were available only in emergencies. I suppose many of us are guided by a criterion, perhaps an unconscious one, of balancing our circumstances against theirs: if they are so pressed that they are always doing without things and if we are sufficiently well-heeled to have a wider range of choices about the things we do, most of us are inclined to share something with them of what we have.

In questions of money we should try to avoid feelings of obligation from the past: "I should have taught him to save." Or guilt feelings: "If only I had been a better father she wouldn't be in this mess." It is best to deal only with the situation as it is now.

Wills and Trusts

Everyone should have a will. Grandparents may wonder, however, whether to bequeath things to their children or to the grandchildren. Specific bequests to individual grandchildren, perhaps a thousand dollars to Julia when she is twenty-one, may be thought of as a nice gesture but, with present-day inflation, the gift may turn out to be disappointingly small by the time the grandchild gets it. In normal circumstances where the parents are able to plan for their children in the best way, I think it best to leave as much as you can to your children rather than to sequester a bit of it for your grandchildren. As parents, your children can then make decisions about using the family's resources to help their children, your grandchildren, in future years.

We have friends whose means are limited, but they have set aside small amounts each year in trust funds for each grandchild to help with university education. Their children, the parents, have good jobs but it appears unlikely that they will earn or accumulate much money. The grandparents give high priority to higher education, and this is their way of doing something about it.

Gifts

What about gifts of money to the grandchildren when you see them? From time to time, of course, as a treat, gifts are fun to give but I advise against doing it regularly. The child quickly learns to expect it and to see it as more important than seeing you again. Should the grandparent give the child an allowance? Certainly not on a regular basis, but perhaps during a summer vacation or in the rare circumstances where the grandparent has to take over the duties and functions of parenting. Allowances should be arranged by the parents as a normal part of teaching children the disciplines of money. It is for the parents to decide how much they can afford to give the children each week. If the parents are too poor even to think about allowances, it is usually best to give the parents what you can.

Money is one thing; a picture, a pretty plate or a ring is something different. If you have some treasured object that your grandchild has admired, give it to her as a souvenir. It will help her remember you and the pleasures you shared.

Gifts are mostly for special occasions, but we may wonder whether to mark such occasions with a tangible toy or with cash. It depends to some extent on age. Most of us have learned that we don't score high points by giving money to a child who does not yet understand what it is for. By the time they get to their teens, however, most grandchildren prefer cash. Best of all is to be in touch with our grandchildren frequently enough to know what they want and what is appropriate. It is never wrong to consult the parents. When grandparents live some distance away there is a lot to be said for sending a check as a birthday present unless we have been given a hint in advance. Children's fads and tastes vary in different places, and so do the styles of clothing. A particular style of shirt may be all the rage where we live but not where they live.

Competition often arises when there are two or more sets of grandparents, each wanting to give as much as the others. Grandma Cecile writes: "There is the natural competition between maternal and paternal grandparents for the love, affection and time of the grandchildren. Jealousy of the other grandparents may be an instinctive emotion, particularly when one pair is closer than the other in time and distance. This unproductive competition may be evidenced by competitive gift giving."

Children are human, and they will negotiate for as much as they can get. More important—and thank goodness for this—they are not dumb. They can tell the difference between rich and poor. They do not withhold their love from a grandparent with limited means in favor of another who lavishes presents.

Competitiveness enters into gift giving among the grandchildren themselves. Grandma Barbara writes about the relationships between her granddaughters and herself regarding gifts. "There is a lot of jealousy between Remmie and her sister, and even now that they are almost twelve and ten years old, I still try to give them identical presents and send equally pretty postcards."

When their ages and tastes are different, is it necessary that presents be of the same value? Grandparents find various solutions. Vi and Al, with ten grandchildren, comment: "We don't give to them all as much as we give to the youngest one." The youngest is their daughter's only child, who has a special place and special needs. They have been partners with their daughter in raising Bobby and have a close emotional attachment. "The other grandchildren have well-to-do families. We give each child a good Christmas gift, which we've saved for and which we buy after consulting their parents. But for Bobby we buy small gifts frequently."

This brings us to presents for Christmas, the festive day that has become centered on gifts. Children become satiated when they get too many elaborate gifts, whether for Christmas or a birthday. The best course is for the grandparents to consult in advance about the gifts, with each other and the parents. Not all gifts need to be wrapped and presented in too large a pile. A grandparent can think carefully about the child's special interests and respond to them with a tape, tickets to the theater, a ball game or a gift certificate from a favorite sports or music shop.

One way I have found to handle Christmas is to take each grandchild window-shopping a few weeks ahead. This activity takes time and energy but it is a highly satisfactory experience. When they are encouraged to talk about values and about how much you can afford to spend, they learn something about establishing their own preferences. I admit that it does not always work so smoothly. I overheard a seven-year-old speaking with her grandmother in the toy department: "Grandma, I want that GI Joe *not* for Christmas, I want it now!" The answer was a firm and sensible negative.

Children occasionally appreciate alternative gifts—such as when you take them to movies, museums, concerts, the theater, ballet, hockey, baseball, soccer or basketball games. One grandmother, after an excursion to the planetarium with two of her grandchildren, remarked: "Middle-class children have so much in their lives that it is not always easy to inspire them with our offerings." She consults them in advance to find out what they have not already seen and what interests them. And she suggests that they bring along one of their friends. It can make the difference between an enthusiastic or boring excursion.

If your hobby is building things, one way to a child's heart is to make Christmas presents. The following is from a letter written by a friend in South Carolina: "My husband, Dick, makes great furniture, and the Christmas before last he made each grandchild a bench. The Christmas before that he made a small box with a brass plate with initials, which make the present more personal. I make sweaters and cushions or whatever with embroidered names or initials or special jams they like. We do these things because we like to, but, looking back, they are the most appreciated presents and do create a special bond.

Another example of this kind was a lovely gift at our fiftieth wedding anniversary. Two of our grandchildren gave us a little Eskimo carving of a beaver mounted on a stand to which they added a small log for the beaver to chew on. This was, no doubt, inspired by their father, whose father had once inspired him along similar lines.

A subtle reflection on the meaning of gift giving comes from Grandma Elaine, who was brought up in England. She writes: "When my two were quite small we were able to stay with the grandparents for two months and had the pleasure of being taken to the seaside for holidays all together, to the same place I had been taken for many years as a child. My grandfather, the only one I knew, had always seemed pleased in a mild way to see his grandchildren (myself and my sister) and handed out half a crown and a peppermint on each visit. When I was an officer in the WAAF during the war, he still gave me a few shillings, which I accepted cheerfully. Years later, when we were there on our summer holidays, Father gave the children an allowance of sixpence on Saturday with the injunction not to spend it all in the same shop. There was not much kissing, et cetera, except good night, but perhaps the gift was the equivalent sign of fondness."

The Value of Money

Grandparents can help young children to learn about money. In teaching a child about this or any other subject, it is important to bear in mind how the child learns. He is unlikely to pay much attention to saving until he begins to think about the future. During his early years he tends to be focused mainly on the present. Were you given a dime bank when you were a kid? What did you do with it? I had several of them at different times, and the story was always the same: the bank did not teach me much. I would put dimes into it when I was prompted to do so. In no time at all I was busting to get the whole wad out to spend it, after which the bank would sit forgotten on a shelf.

Children learn about the future only gradually as their experience accumulates. A young boy may want a bike more than anything else in the world. He can be encouraged to save dimes and quarters if the grandparents offer to make up the difference between the cost of the bike and the amount he has saved. The bike will then mean more to him when the great day comes. The thing is to let him pay for part of it out of his small accumulation.

In the ordinary course of living, our grandchildren hear us ask about prices and they see us pay for what we buy. We help them thus to learn about money. By the gifts we select, we tell them something about us and about how we see them. They get to know quite a lot about our wherewithal and what we do with it, and we can choose what sort of an example we wish to set. We help them find out how to live and, very important, that money is a tool and not an end in itself.

11

Special Problems

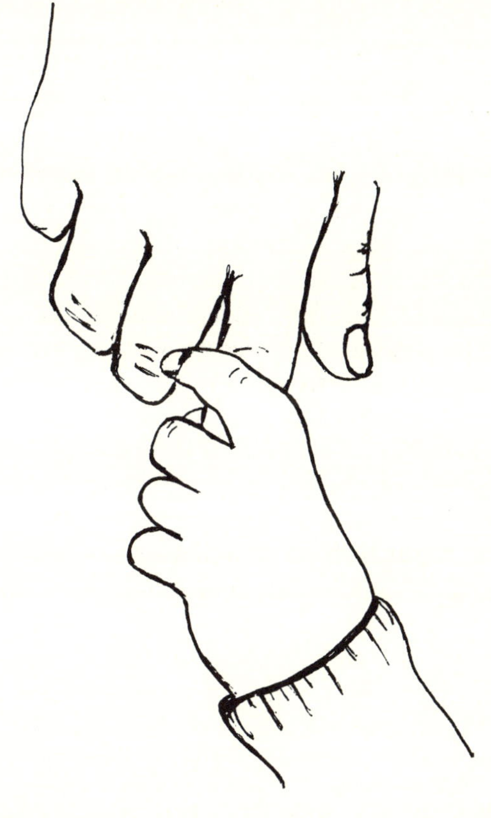

Seeking Access

It is hard to accept, but some parents deny grandparents access to their grandchildren. This occurs more frequently than most of us would like to believe. It is made even more painful by what it signifies about the relations between grandparents and parents. Some of the parents who deny access are still children themselves, fearful of their children's grandparents, and of their concern and advice. They may reject the older generation, especially their in-laws, for a number of reasons. Divorced parents may also deny access to their in-laws, associating the spouse's parents with what they perceive as the damage done by the spouse. Grandparents have a hard time with divorce anyway, and when access is denied in this way, it is even more stressful.

A member of the Grand Society—Grandparents Requesting Access and Dignity—was quoted as saying: "Forty percent of the cases in which access is denied are the result of estrangement between the grandparents and their own children, not as the result of divorce or separation of the parents." Other reasons for parents wanting to avoid contact with grandparents might include sexual abuse, brainwashing and kidnapping. With one young mother it was not that she wanted to stay separated from her family. Rather, she had become involved in a cult that forbids family contact.

Parents who deny access may not clearly understand the needs of the grandparents to be with their grandchildren and their children's needs to be with their grandparents. Lacking perspective or peripheral vision, they may be too immersed in their own life or too clouded by resentment to see the importance of the relationship between grandparents and grandchildren. But they belong together. A grandchild carries, in her little body, a quarter of each of her grandparents' genes, and sometimes some recognizable common features. Grandchildren need a relationship with their grandparents in order to explore their heritage and identity.

Separation and lack of access are agonizing when we know the children are within reach. Some grandparents have, however, been able to get effective help. The procedure is delicate and requires sensitive professional advice.

In Ontario the Children's Law Reform Act of 1983 provides for parents and people other than natural parents (which includes grandparents) to have access. Grandparents can apply to the Family Court for an order for access. Because this involves a confrontational legal approach, grandparents may be hesitant to resort to it. The existence of the law serves to make clear to the parents that grandparents have rights and that access is not solely a question of parental discretion.

There is also a program of counseling and mediation attached to the Provincial Court's Family Division. I am told by a social worker attached to this program that some parents resist grandparental access for specific reasons, founded or unfounded. They may worry that grandparents will overindulge the children, that they will denigrate their daughter-in-law to the children or that they will be unreasonable about visiting times. Caught in such a situation a grandparent could put forward a reasonable and specific proposal, promise to stick to it and later make sure to do so.

If anyone doubts the strength of a grandparent's emotional connection with grandchildren, they should look at Argentina. Grandparents there are asserting their continuing attachments to their families and their rights to realize them. Their expressions are powerful and poignant. At noontime in Buenos Aires, day after day, hundreds of older women gather in the city square to demonstrate their resolve to find their grandchildren.

They are the mothers of the Lost Generation, thousands of whom disappeared, along with their young children, during the previous corrupt regime, which brooked no critics. Anyone who failed to agree with the government could be taken by the secret police, tortured and eventually killed. The children of those killed were treated as anonymous foundlings and farmed out for adoption, mainly to members of the political establishment and the army.

With more freedom of expression under the present government, members of the older generation have put forward their strong demands. With help from abroad, governmental commissions and forensic scientists are engaged in tracing and identifying the children of the Lost Generation. The vigilant grandmothers parade every day to keep the search going. The Argentina grandmothers demonstrate the profound trauma of families torn asunder by separation.

Child Abuse

Child abuse used not to be spoken about, and was only rarely reported. Efforts are now being made by medical authorities, law-enforcement agencies and child and family services to bring it into the open. Because it is now more likely to be reported, it seems to be on the increase. Whether it is cannot be determined. Statistics are not reliable.

Child abuse is malevolent and frequent. It may consist of neglect, physical assault, sexual molestation or psychological invasion. It may occur between different family members—between siblings, between parent and child or between grandparent and child. Other close family members or friends can also be involved.

Grandparents whose lives have been touched and hurt by this problem are full of conflicting feelings. In addition to fear and anger, they may feel impotent that they can do so little. They may feel guilt, especially if they are the ones to report the abuse to the authorities; they may be torn between conflicting loyalties to the adult child and the grandchild; and they may feel helpless if they are unable to get assistance.

Any suspicion you have regarding abuse should be looked into. Do not dismiss a child's fears or your own intuition. Talk, if you can, to the grandchild's parents. If they refuse to take action, you may have to go to the authorities, hard as that may be.

The following are three cases reported to me from the head social worker of a large metropolitan hospital:

In the first case the grandmother was looking after her grandchild, the child of her son and his common-law wife. The wife was claiming welfare illegally, and threatened to take the child away if the grandmother told the welfare worker that she (the grandmother) was not receiving rent from the couple. The mother beat the child when the grandmother was not around. The grandmother was torn between fear of more harm to her grandchild if she forced the couple out and her own failing health and inability to cope. The son was not an ally in getting help or clarifying the situation.

In the second case the grandfather was sexually molesting his sixteen-year-old granddaughter, who ran away to stay with a relative. Grandfather refused to continue to support her (which he had been doing since her father died) if she did not return to him. The relative was afraid to inform the Children's Aid Society for fear of repercussions. The granddaughter was, of course, reluctant to expose her grandfather.

In another case the grandmother tried to get the Children's Aid Society to protect her grandson, who was being abused by her son-in-law. Her daughter was so terrified of her husband, who was beating her, that she could do nothing, and she refused to testify against him. The Children's Aid Society investigated but could not get enough hard evidence to take the child away. Later, they failed to act on medical evidence, which the grandmother informed them of (broken bones and bruises), and the child died at his father's hand.

I have used extreme examples drawn from hospital experience. There are many cases of minor abuse that could become serious. Maltreatment of our grandchildren is a very sensitive problem, and we should not hesitate to do something about it. Calling your local Children's Aid Society is a good place to start.

Biological Grandparents

"Birth grandparents" is the name given to grandparents who have lost their grandchildren through adoption. Many, usually young, mothers give their children up for adoption. Often these mothers have lived at home with their babies, to whom the grandparents become very attached. Even when grandparents agree that adoption is the right decision, emotional trauma cannot be dismissed. The grandmother grieves along with her daughter. The original identity of an adopted child has been safeguarded as secret in most jurisdictions, but there's a growing tendency to loosen these restrictions to some extent. Some birth parents have succeeded in meeting the child's adoptive parents, and the contact opens up new possibilities for them. The procedure is not recommended for all, and professional guidance is a prerequisite.

The Disabled Child

When a baby is born with an impairment, either mental or physical, the parents know about it right away and grandparents soon after. All of them are shocked and disappointed. From then on they are in it together and looking at a long road ahead.

The doctor may tell them there is some hope of alleviating the problem, now or later, and a blessed remedial process begins to work. There are community services to be consulted about the condition and things to be learned. People always feel better when there is some hope for the future or at least something useful to be done. Parents and grandparents begin to think about the money, time, caring and sharing that are going to be required.

Things get better still as they all begin to discover that the baby is a human being like others. The impairment is there, but he is not just an impairment. He is warm and alive; he reaches out for succor and responds in his own way. The adults' feelings of shock—not unmixed with rejection—begin to melt away as they respond to him as a person.

The costs of looking after a handicapped child are considerable. Grandparents are usually willing, if necessary, to reach to the bottoms of their barrels to help. With regard to time, a disabled child needs a lot of it and will continue to do so. Grandparents can arrange to spend time with the child.

Community services vary from one city or town to another, and in Canada they tend to be pretty good. Grandparents should make sure the parents of the child are in touch with appropriate services. Qualified services are professionally staffed to handle physical and psychological problems, children with cerebral palsy or mental retardation, crippled children, blind children and the hard of hearing. There are also child and family clinics for emotionally disturbed children.

My husband suffered a serious physical impairment at the age of six, and he has a few thoughts to share on the subject. He thinks it useful for parents and grandparents to be aware that the child has a different view than theirs of what is going on. He remembers, at about the time of his first major operation, overhearing his doctor tell his parents in an undertone that he had little chance to survive. But how does a child of six react to a thing like death, especially when he is having a hard time anyway? Less seriously than he would later, when he has a few thoughts about the future. Although the news of his impending demise did not mean much to him at the time, he most emphatically did not want to see his parents cry. He remembers assuring them that everything was going to be all right.

Care and service are essential but, in the longer run, motivation is more important to the disabled child. My husband's heaviest load of adjustment came in preadolescence and in the teens. People were attentive to him, but he was always aware of being alien and different. Many physically disabled children are similarly aware of themselves, and they either come through to the other side of it or they fail. They can choose to make the best of what they have or they can put chips on their shoulders and continue always to look for special help.

My husband feels that his older family members had some understanding of this and helped direct him. His grandmother, Nana, was the one who made him feel there was nothing very important that he couldn't at least try to do. He feels now that he has gone a good many miles on faulty equipment, and he wants to put his thanks to Nana into my book on grandparents.

Invalid Grandparents

Grandchildren with invalid grandparents living in their houses are pressured on several counts. Space may be one problem—perhaps two children have had to move in together to give Grandpa his own bedroom. Noise level is another tender issue, as are chores related to the nursing care. Then there is the lack of freedom for their friends to visit comfortably. On the positive side, the opportunity to help look after an elderly grandparent can bring satisfaction to some children.

Ill or disabled grandparents can become special problems (see Chapter Five) but on the whole, the problems that come with aging are normal and universal.

However, with grandparents who are really out of touch with reality, for example if they have Alzheimer's disease, or with those who are depressed or painfully ill, family life is very hard. Children find it difficult to understand the facts of this kind of trouble and the resulting separation from them. Parents, perhaps, can do no more than remind their concerned children of the good times they have had with a grandparent in the past and that such illnesses and eventually death do come to us all. Sharing the facts of the illness with children may help them to accept with confidence that the problem is under control and that they are not in any way responsible for it.

Alcoholism is another major problem for grandparents and grandchildren. Mental-health counselors can do much to relieve the stress that such a problem brings to a family. Whether the grandparent or the parent is the victim of the disease, your grandchildren are seriously involved. But there is help and help should be sought. (See Chapter Twelve, Resources.)

A grandchild who has been lovingly attended by a grandparent during his childhood will be responsive to a grandparent's special needs in old age. Simple responses like checking to make sure Grandma has turned the oven off or locked the door for the night or turned off her lamp before she fell asleep are little tasks willingly and often spontaneously accepted by older children. A caring attitude comes full cycle.

12

Resources

Yesterday's grandmother was on hand. Today's may have to fly thousands of miles to greet a new grandchild. In attempting to be on closer terms with grandchildren, our resources are taxed, and we need to tap some new ones. We are stretched beyond the models of old-time grandparents.

Inner Resources

Primarily, we grandparents need instant intuition and long-distance telepathy. We need flexibility and sensitivity, an attitude of openness and objectivity. These are fine words but responding in practice to our young families requires more than words. Of course, we may find the very thought of being old enough to be a grandparent off-putting.

Turning our back on the challenge of grandparenting, in the hope of picking up the threads later on, is perhaps the most obvious false move we could make. We can all relate to the desire to keep our distance and let our children manage, but grandparents who place a block between themselves and their grandchildren now will find their later relationships with their grandchildren stiff and unfulfilling.

Most of us are looking forward to our new status and are reaching to enrich our lives with these new connections and seek resources for the job.

First of all, we need trust—in our children and ourselves. Advice to our grown children can be received as criticism and create a chilling relationship. Trust your grown child. Yes, your daughters and sons will make mistakes in raising their children. Didn't you? Learning to be a parent takes trial and error. Grandparents can't do it for them. Keep your relationship comfortably resourceful, not possessive.

Grandparents also need their own inner resources. At times when we are hurt or shocked by developments in the young family, we cannot expect them to help us or to organize their lives to suit us. We can only be in control of ourselves and not our adult children. A grandparent with inner strengths of his own is of more use to his offspring than a meddler. No one can prescribe such resources for others, but we all have them, in the form of religious values or beliefs in freedom and self-respect.

Other resources most likely to be helpful are the grandchildren themselves; the parents, with all their love and understanding; friends; and other grandparents, with their diverse experiences, community resources and books and publications.

Our Grandchildren

How many times have we seen a grandmother reaching over a school-yard fence, following the play of young children or observing nursery-school children taking turns on a slide? At a distance, we are observing developing characters as they relate to their fellow playmates. If it is our own grandchild we are watching, there is a thrill in seeing his special alertness or his tentative approach to some challenge. Knowing our grandchild directly, through observation, through playing with him and nurturing him is our best resource.

Most of us could bone up on the ages and stages and learn a bit more about our grandchildren's interests and how some of our interests relate to theirs. We can explore with them; we can write to them and encourage them to write to us. This is how we know our friends, and our grandchildren are our friends.

Our Grandchildren's Parents

From the first glow of presenting to us our new grandchild, the parents are the most reliable source of appreciation and interpretation of our grandchild. Their knowledge is superior. As our grandchildren grow and mature, we may or may not live close by. We depend on our adult children and their spouses as primary resources to keep us in touch with them.

Our very best interpretations of our grandchildren are their parents or stepparents.

Friends and Other Grandparents

Invite your neighbors in when your grandchildren are with you, to share some special skills. Take part in discussions with other grandparents to become clued in to imaginative ways of relating to these little dynamos of activity. Grandma Betty reported an experiment she carried out over a period of weeks with her granddaughters. With a group of friends, they tried out food in small cafés of different national origins and bought some of the foods to cook at home. It was an experiment, Betty said, that went over well. Bob talked about enthusiasm for a joint venture to the apple farm of friends of his. Some other grandparents got together to visit a local lumberyard with their grandchildren to purchase materials for a joint project, making toy boats, bookends and sundry other unrecognizable wooden objects.

We can also take some hints from friends about how not to bore children. Long speeches do; talking over their heads does; talking to others while pretending to talk to them does. If you stop to think, you and your friends will have many more examples of how we bore children.

Community Resources

Beyond the immediate relatives and extended family, the resource potential of our community is often neglected. Here is a list of organizations and programs that are suitable for both parents and grandparents. Parents are often too busy to make use of some of them, but grandparents just might have time.

Public libraries Use them with your grandchild. Take time to let your grandchild wander through her section of the library and choose some books to take home. Make a note of special child-centered library programs advertised on the library bulletin board, as well as announcements of other community events and activities for children and adults.

Museums, art galleries, science and nature centers These have infinite resources available to intrigue grandchildren. Often there are classes.

Neighborhood parks and playgrounds See listings in the telephone directory under Parks and Recreation for your area. Refer to your local community information center to find your way to information about location and programs such as ski areas, public swimming pools, nature walks and other community programs. The government pamphlets on heritage areas are of special interest.

Nature walks and neighborhood excursions Try both organized nature hikes and grandparent-initiated walks (beaches, woods, trails, city streets and so on). Your neighborhood may be full of new discoveries for your grandchildren. If, however, there is danger involved in heavy traffic in the area, think twice about where to walk. Stick to areas where you can feel relaxed on these excursions. Some neighborhoods have beautiful gardens; some have shopping centers with play equipment or puppet shows or original drama; some have lumberyards. A high-rise office elevator ride can be a new and thrilling experience for a grandchild.

Music You can have music wherever you go: singing together in the car as you drive along, listening to records, discs or tapes at music stores, going to an outdoor band concert, an indoor symphony concert or a dance program. One lovely combination of seniors and children and music came about in an elementary school where an intergenerational program had already developed between the school and a seniors' home in the neighborhood. A choir leader, after rehearsing the two choirs separately and developing connections by letter, brought the two of them together for a concert in a worthy cause. This program might suggest ideas to other grandparents.

Festivals from around the world is a theme of many local community fetes at holiday time. Music and dance abound. Caribbean festival time is a spectacle to behold as are many other national group occasions. Take advantage of them. With your grandchildren. Libraries, museums, art galleries and music halls also present many happy musical events.

Immigration offices These offices have a host of relevant pamphlets to help orient immigrant grandparents or families into a new community. These include material regarding health care, social services, recreation and other concerns. Phone your local community information center or call the immigration office.

Governments National, provincial and state governments publish pamphlets for parents that are of interest to grandparents as well. One such, which keeps being updated, is "A Guide for Parents of Young Children." They also publish other pamphlets and books relevant to family life.

Drop-in centers There are drop-in centers for parent (or grandparent) and child. These are sometimes called family resource centers, children's storefront, support groups, or family connections. There are also programs at the YMCA, senior citizens' centers, churches and synagogues. These programs have sprung up in communities, some professionally staffed and some led by trained volunteers. They provide a setting where parents and grandparents can discuss common concerns and the children play in a safe supervised play area.

Such opportunities for communication among parents, grandparents, staff and children can provide interesting reminders of how to play and talk with children and how to appreciate normal childhood growth and development. Grandparents can gain from *and* give to groups of this kind.

Day care Call your local community information center.

Bulletin boards Look for these in schools, shopping centers, drop-in centers, community centers, clubs, libraries, and at the Y. Use them for information and to communicate with other grandparents.

Meals on Wheels There are different telephone numbers for different areas of Metro Toronto as in other communities. A connection with this organization might enable you to invite a grandchild to visit you without putting undue pressure on you or the grandchild. This is not to suggest that the grandchild be served by Meals on Wheels, but that you might be in a better mood to relax and talk with your grandchild without the worry or fatigue of preparing your midday meal.

Public Health Department This department issues pamphlets on various health topics. Grandparents find them useful for themselves and for reference for family use. Phone the department for referral on topics of concern.

Advocacy Center for the Elderly Hundreds of grandparents are suffering a subtle form of emotional abuse, and any legislative change that would improve access of noncustodial parents could improve the lot of grandparents. The Ontario government, via the Attorney General's Ministry committee on family law enforcement, is reviewing the legislation and looking at better ways of enforcing orders made by the court. (Refer to local institutions)

Grand Society (Grandparents Requesting Access and Dignity). The aims of the Grand society are support systems; best interest of the child; mediation; public education; prevention through family life education; and changes in the law to allow specific recognition of grandparents.

Senior citizens' organizations and centers See your Yellow Pages or community information center.

Volunteer grandparents Churches, synagogues, schools

and other organizations run programs for children without grandparents. Many children do not know their grandparents. Sometimes children just attach themselves to an older next-door neighbor because they like the feel of these older people and the fact that they have time to give them.

Some schools use grandparents to help with projects in arts and crafts, photography, music, pottery, weaving and gardening. Grandparents can have a soothing effect on hyperactive children.

Senior citizens can become very creative in the community, helping to meet the needs of these children, volunteering in day-care centers, drop-in centers and in senior citizens' organizations.

Colleges, universities and high schools Many schools run adult education courses for seniors. Request a course on grandparenting. Such a course has been presented in more than one Ontario college.

Foster Grandparents Write to Action, Washington, D.C., 20525. In the United States there are more than 18,000 men and women officially designated under a federally financed program. They tend to work four-hour shifts, five days a week, and perform typical grandparenting functions—dressing and bathing infants, reading to toddlers, going on walks, playing catch, working at carpentry with kids, and listening to children. Four-year-old Betty said: "I do have a Grannie now".

The Foundation for Grandparenting Write to 10 West Hyatt Ave., Mt. Kisco, N.Y., 10549. In the United States grandparents may petition their state courts for visitation rights otherwise denied them by members of their own family or others. "This foundation is dedicated to the three-generation family and to encouraging intergenerational relationships between children and older persons." They publish a newsletter, *The Vital Connection*, and operate a grandparent network with many branches.

National Federation of Parents and Friends of Gays
5715 16th Street NW, Washington, D.C., 20011.

In Our Home

Music Enjoy as much music as you and your grandchildren feel comfortable with. Call a halt to endless noise but learn to listen to their favorite artists. It will put you in a special class of "with-it" grandparents. Play instruments, records, tapes, radio, and sing around the piano or by the fireplace. Happy times!

Tapes Tape recorders, even inexpensive ones, can allow children to record stories, speeches and music, and send them to grandparents. And grandparents can record stories and events of the past and the present that will be treasured later on by grandchildren.

The computer If you have one in your home, your grandchildren will delight in using it. Ours composed our nicest 50th Wedding Anniversary card on it, complete with drawings and decorations. Grandpa Ken developed on his word processor a story which his ten-year-old grandson had composed in typical ten-year-old short sentences and printed it in the bi-monthly magazine which he edits and produces. Nice cooperative effort!

Baby sitters Keep a list on your telephone pad of baby sitters and teen-age friends. They can be called upon to inject some energy into activities with visiting grandchildren when you are fatigued. They can supply extra resources in areas where you are less competent or confident.

Equipment pool Keep a list at your house of other grandparents who might share baby equipment and toys for short periods of time when your or their grandchildren come visiting. You might even be the organizer of such a pool.

Activity file Keep a running file entitled, "What are we going to do today?" Clip out ideas from newspaper stories or note suggestions from friends that may slip your mind later.

Letters, postcards, tapes These can tell the stories of recent exciting adventures you have had. One grandmother I know, out of correspondence with her granddaughter, has started a jointly authored book with drawings as well as text.

Exploring special sights in or from your house or apartment You can use binoculars to see skaters on the neighborhood rink or playground activity; pick out the makes of cars on the road below; do some bird watching; watch a parade and lots more. You can enjoy the garden together, if not as gardeners at least as an easy place to sit and talk or play a game or swing or play paper boats in a puddle from last night's rain. Of course if there is an attic in your house, there are hidden treasures to be explored.

Family pictures Photographs and slides with family background commentary provide much interest and hilarity.

Sharing skills Sewing, knitting, craft work, carpentry, housekeeping are occupations to encourage new interests and conversation. It's amazing how some kids love to make beds away from home.

Play "Grandchildren never seem to tire of playing games—all kinds of games adjusted to their age level which give them a sense of accomplishment and easy competition," said Grandma Margaret. "In addition to card and board games we keep a set of construction blocks with cars and trucks and planes for free play as well as a box of dress-up clothes and a set of tiny family dolls." Grandparents can become more than baby sitters. "We are special friends who have fun together," said Grandma Bronwyn.

Reading, telling stories and having books around are especially fine resources for grandparents to share with grandchildren.

Appropriate TV

Food is at the top of most grandchildren's interests when they visit grandparents. Just when grandparents are taking dieting more seriously it can be hard to serve grandchildren their favorite dishes (you know, hot dogs, potato chips, chocolate ice cream, cookies). An easy way to attract children to different kinds of food is to serve Chinese style—put bowls of food out and let them help themselves. Be sure to serve *some* of their specials and remember, we all like bananas.

Travel day trips, over-night trips or longer trips.

Books

Arnstein, Helene S. *Between Mothers-in-Law & Daughters-in-Law: Achieving a Successful and Caring Relationship.* New York: Dodd Mead, 1985.

Cherlin, Andrew J. and Frank F. Furstenberg. *The New American Grandparent.* New York: Basic Books, 1986.

Dodson, Fitzhugh with Paula Reuben. *How to Grandparent.* New York: Harper and Row, 1981. With an elaborate appendix on books, toys and play materials.

Farber, Norma. *Grandma and Grandpa Are Special People.* Toronto: Stoddard, 1984. Children writing about grandparents.

Galinsky, Ellen and Judy David. *The Preschool Years: Family Strategies That Work—From Experts and Parents.* New York: Times Books, 1988.

Jolly, Hugh. *Grandparents' Handbook.* London: Pagoda Books, 1984. A practical guide of things to do with very young grandchildren.

Kornhaber, Arthur. *Between Parents and Grandparents.* New York: St. Martins, 1986. An exploration of the emotional bond between grandchildren and grandparents, analysing problems such as family feuds, remote or long distance grandparents and competing grandparents.

Kornhaber, Arthur and K.L. Woodward. *Grandparents Grandchildren: The Vital Connection.* New York: Doubleday, 1981. Link between grandparents and grandchildren, based on interviews with grandchildren and grandparents (300 each).

Kresny, Laurence and Marc Brown. *Dinosaurs Divorce*. Boston: Atlantic Monthly Press, 1988.

Leach, Penelope. *Your Baby and Child: from birth to five*. New York: Alfred A. Knopf Inc., 1978.

Leshan, Eda. *Grandparents: A Special Kind of Love*. New York: Macmillan, 1986.

Messinger, Lillian. *Re-marriage is a Family Affair*. New York: Plenum Press, 1984.

Minden, Harold A. *Two Hugs for Survival: Strategies for Effective Parenting*. Toronto: McClelland and Stewart, 1982.

Pollock, Sandra and Jeanne Vaughn. *Politics of the Heart: A Lesbian Parenting Anthology*. New York: Firebrand Books, 1987. Has an extensive bibliography of books and articles discussing custody and parenting issues.

Rafkin, Louis. *Different Daughters*. Pittsburgh: Cleis Press, 1987. A book by mothers of lesbians.

Shedd, Charles. *Then God Created Grandparents and It Was Very Good*. New York: Doubleday, 1976.

Staybough, Charles. *The Grandparents' Catalogue*. New York: Doubleday, 1986. Lists hundreds of projects, activities and books for grandparents and grandchildren.

Wallerstein, Judith S. and Sandra Blakeslee. *Second Chances, Men, Women and Children: A Decade after Divorce*. New York: Ticknor and Fields, 1989.

Wasserman, Selma. *Longdistance Grandmother*. Vancouver: Hartley and Marks, 1988.

Index